SAME DUDE DIFFERENT NAME

BY: MISS E

Inspired by all the people who said I couldn't do it;
Dedicated to those who are not afraid to learn and heal
from their mistakes.

☺ You are making a difference by purchasing this book, as a portion of all proceeds will be donated to help victims of domestic violence ☺

Copyright © 2025 Miss E.

All rights reserved. No part of this publication may be reproduced, distributed, or transmitted in any form or by any means, including photocopying, recording, or other electronic or mechanical methods, without the prior written permission of the publisher, except in the case of brief quotations embodied in critical reviews and certain other noncommercial uses permitted by copyright law. For permission requests, write to the publisher, addressed "Attention: Permissions Coordinator," at the following email address: gardenofe143@gmail.com

ISBN: (Paperback)

Any references to historical events, real people, or real places are used fictitiously. Names, characters, and places are products of the author's imagination.

Front cover image by Redd Ryan.

Printed in the United States of America.

UMM HMM LLC
Lodi, NJ 07644
www.umm-hmm.com

Table of Contents

Introduction: Find Strength From Within To Better Your Own Life And, In Turn, Inspire Others... v

Chapter One: Daddy's Little Girl: How It All Began 1
Lesson Learned: The Past Molds Who a Person Is

Chapter Two: She Needed Her Father, But He Needed The Lotto.................. 6
Lesson Learned: Never Hurt Yourself to Help Someone Else, Even If It Is Your Family

Chapter Three: "Just Perfect" Joseph.. 19
Lesson Learned: Nice Guys Sometimes Finish Last

Chapter Four: Notorious Nate.. 24
Lesson Learned: Words Can Hurt As Much As Fists

Chapter Five: Horrible Hector.. 44
Lesson Learned: Think Before Making Life-Changing Decisions

Chapter Six: The Crooked O 51
Lesson Learned: Gay Men Can Appear Straight

Chapter Seven: Terrible Tyler... 60
Lesson Learned: Bad Boys Get What They Want If You Let Them

Chapter Eight: Victorious Vincent 85
Lesson Learned: Some Things Aren't As Good As They Appear To Be

Chapter Nine: Not So Kind Keith 90
Lesson Learned: Making The Wrong Person Fall In Love With You Means Nothing

Chapter Ten: Two-Timing Todd 97
Lesson Learned: Cheaters Never Win

Chapter Eleven: Slim Pickings 133
Lesson Learned: Be Picky, Be Very Picky!

Chapter Twelve: Karma.. 147
Lesson Learned: Karma Is Crazy, It Feels Good and Hurts At The Same Time

Chapter Thirteen: A Chapter For The Men of The World 150

INTRODUCTION

Find strength from within to better your own life and, in turn, inspire others

A m I who I really want to be?

My sister's friend once said that her mom kissed a lot of frogs before finding her prince. I responded by saying, "I have sex froggy style with lingerie and high heels and still can't find my prince." I learned that is because the more I would try, the worse it would be. It gave men the impression I would accept anything (which I did) and that I had no self-esteem (which I didn't). I have learned to just sit back and let things go where they are meant to. I NEVER try too hard anymore. If a guy doesn't like me for who I am, he will not like me more if I put on lingerie or have the best sex ever with him. The men I dated in the past may have liked me for the moment, but they would be with me to try to use me for whatever they could get, whether it was money, sex, an ego boost, a place to stay, and the list goes on. They had no respect for me because I was showing them through my actions that I had no respect for myself. I am keeping my dresser full of lingerie for someone special when the time is right; Someone who appreciates me and deserves ALL of me; Someone who will go out of his way as much as I have gone out of my way and who won't complain about doing it because he likes to see me happy.

I remember being in college and a professor giving the class the following assignment: Write a letter to an ex who has been bribing you and accomplish the following goals with the letter: 1: stop the bribe and 2: make your ex know that you do not want to get back with them. Being a good student and a good writer, I thought to myself, "This is a great assignment!"

So, I went home and came up with the following letter after about 10 minutes:

Your Ex-Girlfriend

123 Not Looking Back Street

New York, New York

My ex-boyfriend

456 Crazy Man Lane

New York, New York

My Response to your Crazy Blackmail:

Dear ex:

I received your letter threatening to blackmail me unless I get back with you. The main reason I broke up with you in the first place was because you would always threaten to blackmail me every time I tried to break up with you. I was myself the whole time I was with you, and

I did not do anything that I would regret. Therefore, there is nothing that I feel you can blackmail me with. If it is pictures that you want to blackmail me with, I am beautiful and I am sure any person who sees any of my pictures would appreciate them more than you seemed to. If it is with words, I know that anyone who knows both of us knows who the honest one is, so I am not the least bit worried. This is just another one of your pathetic attempts to get me back. The only difference is now that I am gone, there is no turning back. I am going to use your words and tell you that you have lost the best thing that ever happened to you. If that is not bad enough, then attempt your desperate measures to blackmail me and make yourself look even worse. I see that you are unhappy over the situation as it is, and I would hate to see you unhappier sitting in jail for harassment, blackmail, or stalking. However, I do have some advice for you, if you choose to take my advice (which is what you should have done a long time ago and we would not have ended up in this situation). You should concentrate your efforts on moving on with your life, leaving me alone, and trying to find someone new. This way, we can both be happy. I decided to take my own advice as well and have moved on to someone else. This will be the first and last response letter that I send to you, as I feel that I made myself clear and am far beyond playing games. You are not even worth this response letter, but it was a requirement for school. Have a nice life.

Sincerely,

Your long-gone ex

When I got to class the following week, we were each given someone else's letter to read and the class had to rate whether each letter accomplished the two goals. My letter was read last, just by coincidence, by a classmate. The class loved the letter and agreed that it had accomplished both goals. One classmate also commented and said that he would "want to run and hide" if he was my ex after reading that letter, and the rest of the class laughed. One girl said, "Wow! I wish I could be like that with my ex. You inspired me." I felt so good about being the star of the class. However, as I walked to the bus that night, I thought to myself, "The attitude I portrayed in my letter is the attitude I want to have when dealing with guys. Instead, I seem desperate and give the wrong men my love...way too much love." From that night on, I made a promise to myself to heal, to be strong, and to stand up for myself in relationships instead of letting people walk all over me. I made a promise to be the person I portrayed in my letter. I made a promise to inspire others to love themselves, to end unhealthy relationships, and to accept only the best treatment from others. And sharing the following story with the world is one way I plan to carry out that promise.

CHAPTER ONE

Daddy's little girl: How it all began

Ember was five years old when her dad picked her up and put her on his shoulders as he was escorted out of their house by police. Her mother was screaming and crying in the background. As they walked through the long hallway that led to the front door, her father told her that he had to leave but that he would always be a part of her life. He told her that since she was the older child, she would oversee taking care of her baby sister from now on, including making sure nothing happened to her. Ember was confused and did not know why he had to leave. She could see that he was upset. She tried her best to be strong and not to cry, although she felt sick to her stomach. Was it her fault he was leaving? Maybe if she had been a better daughter he would've stayed. Little did she know that this day was the beginning of triangulation, narcissistic abuse, and a torn family. Ember had a big task ahead of her: to take care of her sister, to make sure her mother was going to be ok, and to try to get her daddy back.

Every night after this, Ember would not be able to sleep. Her room was near the kitchen and her mom would be up late taking care of her infant sister while crying. One night, Ember began to cry, and her mom came into her bedroom to see what was wrong. Ember asked her why her dad had left them. Her mother hugged her and said it would be ok. She told Ember that she loved her very much and that her dad did too, but that it just wasn't working out, so he had to leave for a while.

Ember quickly came up with a plan to try to fix the situation. She decided to do the best she could in school, to take care of her sister and mother, and to clean up the house all the time. She thought by doing all these things, her dad would surely come back home.

One night, to keep her promise and make sure her sister was safe, Ember leaned into her cradle to give her a kiss. To Ember's surprise, her sister flew out of the cradle, hit the wall, and had blood coming from her face. Her mom came running into the room screaming, picked the baby up, and called 911. Her mother yelled at her and Ember felt horrible. Ember began to get ready to go with her to the hospital. Her mother told Ember that she had done enough and that she would be staying home with her grandmother. Ember cried all night; afraid her sister would never make it back home. Instead of taking care of her, she may have killed her. She was sick to her stomach and wanted to die. Thankfully, her sister returned from the hospital the following day. She had a fractured skull but would be ok. Ember felt relieved. Although Ember was envious of her for being the baby and not having all the responsibility she had, Ember loved her sister more than anything.

When they would have company over, Ember felt as though everyone would give her sister all the attention because she was cute and little. There were a few times when Ember would put on her ballet and jazz costumes and dance in the middle of the living room floor, begging for everyone's attention. She began to be very loud as a child in a desperate attempt to get people to notice her.

As her sister grew older, Ember always kept her promise of keeping her sister safe. She would walk with her to and from school every day and made sure no one messed with her. She would make sure to hold her head every time they wrestled so she did not get hurt. She always let her sister beat her at everything to make her feel good. She was tough on her sister when it came to learning. Her sister knew how to read and write way before she started school. Ember would always let her sister play with her toys. Their mom and grandmother raised them in a single-parent household. Their mother never had a boyfriend because she concentrated on raising the two of them to be strong, independent women.

Their father would visit them every weekend and take them on vacation every now and then. He had girlfriends throughout their childhood. Every time Ember met one of his girlfriends, she would hate them, thinking they were trying to take the place of her mother.

It didn't take long before Ember realized that her father was never coming home. Before long, every time he picked them up, he began complaining about having to pay child support. He would say that their mother and grandmother robbed him and should pay him back. He would tell them to ask their mother for the money back because it should be spent on Ember and her sister. As a child, Ember wanted to believe her dad. After all, her mom never bought them anything special with this money. One day, Ember and her sister decided to confront their mother about this. When they did, she was very angry. She screamed at them and asked them how they thought they had a house and food to eat. She explained how she worked hard to provide for them and that their dad was an "abusive asshole." This was the beginning of her mom's various breakdowns. She would frequently break down by screaming, cursing, and crying. Every time this happened, Ember would shield her sister and take her downstairs to their grandmother's house so they wouldn't have to be subjected to this.

For the rest of Ember's childhood, she was torn between her parents. On one side, her father told her that her mother was a thief, which was very scary to a child. On the other side, her mother would tell her that her father was a gambler. Her mother would ask, "Why else would I leave your father with two small children?" Her mom said that her grandmother worked cleaning on her hands and knees to save money to buy the house they lived in. She was an immigrant and started with nothing. Her dad said that it was his house, and her grandmother was a "selfish bitch" for not letting him live in her part of the house. Ember did not know who or what to believe. Ember often was overwhelmed with feelings of guilt, shame, and anxiety. It was too much for a young girl to have to endure. Despite all she was feeling and going through, Ember kept her promise of doing well in school, even after she realized her dad wasn't coming home. It was a way for her to get attention from others and it felt good. Ember received first honors throughout all her years of school. She was quiet and pleasant in class.

She would only be loud at home. Her friends would come over and say, "Wow, you are like a different person at home. You are so quiet in school." She had no idea that her sister would suffer from her over-achievements. Every time her sister excelled to the next grade, she would have to hear, "Your sister was such a great student." Her sister later told her that she was not able to be herself because she always felt as though she had to follow in Ember's footsteps. Ember would sometimes try to dim her light because she felt guilty for how her sister felt about being compared to her.

Ember was a nerd in school. The "cool" kids would make fun of her and call her ugly. Her class once read a story about a girl named Tall Tina. She enjoyed the story until her classmates began calling her Tall Tina. They would say "How is the air up there, Tall Tina?" Even though they hurt Ember's feelings, and she could find something wrong about each of them, she did not want to say anything back to hurt their feelings. Why would she want to make someone feel bad? So, she kept all this anger inside. Would anyone ever love Ember for her?

CHAPTER TWO

She needed her father, but he needed the lotto

One day, Ember was at a financial training for work. The speaker began talking about reasons why people have financial problems. The speaker said it is what she calls "The D's of financial problems," which include things like divorce and death. Ember couldn't help but add to the list, so she turned around to the guy next to her and said, "Yeah, and Dumbass Dudes." He began cracking up laughing. Ember laughed too but, little did her co-worker know, she was being serious. It was sad but true. Most of the bills Ember had stemmed from being kind to the wrong people. All her life, she supported her father's gambling addiction by putting up with all the emotional abuse and letting him use her for money. This same behavior ended up seeping over to the way she was with the men in her life. As the daughter of a gambler, Ember found herself wanting to please people and help them out financially or any other way she could so that they would like her. It took her almost twenty years to learn that people should like her for her. It may sound ridiculous to some of you reading this book, but to Ember, it was a harsh reality. She was trying to prove to others that she was a good person when she didn't have to because it showed. She gave others money that she needed to survive just so that they would be ok. Ember wasn't really helping anyone. Instead, she was hurting herself.

Ever since she started working, her dad would ask her for money. He would say he paid for Ember all her life through child support, and it was only right for Ember to begin helping him. Without ever asking him what he needed the money for, Ember would just give it to him. He would tell her that he was the father, and she should always "respect thy father." It was a terrible, scary feeling being an adolescent and growing up thinking that her dad would be homeless or hungry if she didn't help. So, Ember did everything she could. She gave him money when he said he needed it. As the years went by, Ember realized she had nothing to show for all her hard work. In fact, she had two and three jobs while going to school to help her dad, even though he didn't seem to appreciate it.

When Ember was 14 years old, she got a job at a pizzeria where her dad used to deliver pizza part time. He said that he got Ember the job (even though she landed the job on her own) and she should give him money because of it. When she was 18, she got kicked out of her mom's house because her mom didn't like her boyfriend at the time. Ember stayed with her boyfriend for about a week until her dad came knocking on his door, begging her to live with him. So, she did, thinking that her father's efforts meant that he cared about her. However, her dad didn't care about her, rather he saw her bad situation as a financial opportunity for himself.

When Ember went to live with her dad and his second wife, she got a job at a party supply store as well as at a restaurant while attending school. Instead of being proud of her hard work and dedication, her dad would constantly put her down. He would say she wasn't good enough. When she told him she wanted to work in law enforcement, he said she didn't have any common sense and would never make it, pointing out that her stepsister was a successful schoolteacher (another successful attempt at triangulation). He would constantly bad mouth Ember's mom. He would say how happy he was with his new wife, how she was so nice to him, and how Ember living there was a burden. Ember thought to herself, "I wasn't the one who asked to live here." In an attempt not to be a burden, she paid rent, bought her own groceries, walked about two miles to and from work each day, took the bus to school, and gave her dad extra money. She was working and did not have a thing to show for it. But she had no real other choice.

When she graduated high school, her dad bought her a new car. The only catch was that she could not have anyone in it. So, Ember drove it for a few months before her dad took it back. He said that she had friends in it when he told her not to. Later, she found out the real reason was because he, in fact, did not buy her the car. His wife did. By the end of their marriage, his ex-wife's once good credit was bad, she was bankrupt, and Ember's dad owed her over $100,000. He blamed Ember for most of the money he owed his ex-wife, saying he would have never borrowed it if it weren't for Ember getting kicked out of her mother's house. Ember couldn't understand why he owed so much money. Her mom always warned her that her dad was a gambler. But was he really? Ember needed to go through more abuse to find out because she wasn't ready to believe the harsh truth yet.

Ember was broke even though she worked day in and day out. As soon as she was old enough, her dad showed her how to open a credit card. It sounded like a good idea, as he said it would help Ember establish good credit for her future. So, she opened her first credit card. She borrowed from this student credit card, which had an extremely high interest rate. She ended up being in even more debt because of following her father's advice. This was the beginning of a big problem. He had Ember open store accounts as well as several other credit cards. He even charged a tennis bracelet for Ember on her account and told her it was her birthday gift. Ember later found out his wife bought her wedding ring for herself as well. It was the beginning of Ember being financially exploited by her father.

Unlike most fathers, Ember's never bought her anything without either asking for it back or making her feel like shit about it. Over time, she started refusing gifts from him because she didn't want to go through torture when he would demand that she give the gift back when he needed the money. After a year of living with him, Ember couldn't take it anymore. Her mom offered to take her back so she went back to live with her mom. Going back was different because Ember was now financially and emotionally destroyed.

Her dad began dating after his divorce from his second wife and needed his own apartment. Ember was at an age when she should have been able to move out on her own and her father should have been helping her. Instead, she gave her father money for his apartment. Shortly after that, he met a woman who began paying his rent. Instead of thanking Ember for helping him, he would tell her how great his new girlfriend was for helping him when no one else would (triangulation at its finest once again). Ember felt used and unappreciated. But she was used to feeling used. When was he going to show her that he loved her?

One Christmas, her father said that he did not have any money to buy anyone gifts. He asked Ember for $300, and she felt bad and gave it to him. To Ember's surprise, he gave her sister a $200 Christmas gift with the money Ember gave him. And what did Ember get? She had tears rolling down her face and pain inside-that's what she got. Ember thought, "Did he love her more than he loved me? Was I really that horrible of a person? Why was he doing this to me?"

Ember maintained two and three jobs for years to help her clean up the mess. She refused to have bad credit. Ember knew she never wanted to be like her dad. He was sick. When she would give him money, he would tell her she was a nice, caring person like him and that she should not be nice to any of her boyfriends because, if she was, they would take advantage of her. Ember thought, "Of course, I should not spend money on them. That would only take away from the money I would give him."

Her dad's addiction was passed onto her sister. Her sister became an alcoholic. She would drink and become a different person. She would steal, was very selfish, and would not help around the house. One day, Ember was upset with her for not helping and being nasty to their mom. So, Ember began yelling at her. Ember's sister picked up the phone and called the police, telling them she was scared for her life. Ember could not believe she did that. Ember had just begun a career in law enforcement. She got so upset after her sister called, that she kicked her.

When the police arrived, Ember's sister realized what she had done so she told them she called by mistake. When they asked Ember what happened, she told them that she kicked her after her sister called them. It just so happened that one of the officers who responded had hit on Ember once before and she did not pay any mind to him. He was disgusting and obnoxious and had gotten the job as a cop only because his father was the chief of police in the town. He also knew where Ember worked and that she would probably lose her job if she were to get arrested. The three officers went outside. When they came back in, he said, "Honesty is your downfall. You are being arrested." They handcuffed Ember and walked her outside to the police car in front of the whole neighborhood. They then took her to headquarters where they handcuffed her to a bench. After a while, she heard a detective who had taken her fingerprints in the past for work, yelling at the other cops and asking why they arrested her. Being that the detective knew Ember, he asked her if she had just put her foot out to try to stop her sister from calling the police or if she had kicked her. He was probably trying to help Ember, but she did not want to lie to the police or anyone else, so she told the truth. The officers ended up calling her job to tell her boss she had been arrested. It was just another example of how one person or event can ruin someone's life. Ember's sister later admitted that she called the police because she was jealous of Ember and her accomplishments and wanted to see her suffer, just like she did in her life.

When the rookie officer drove Ember home, he said, "You should have told us you were a sister officer." Ember replied, "I don't use my job to get me out of anything." Ember started to get her things together when he dropped her off home, and he said, "You don't have to leave the house. It is all over. You can stay here." Ember quickly said, "No, I am going to a hotel until I figure out where I am going to live." This was just a sign that she had to leave. She told the officer, "I would have left sooner but I'm not financially stable because I chose to help everyone else instead of helping myself." The officer said, "It is raining outside. I wish I had someone who would put you up for the night." Ember said, "I am going to a hotel." He replied, "Don't you need a reservation?" Ember wanted to laugh. How sheltered was he? She wasn't staying at the Ritz Carlton. She told him she didn't need a reservation. She was going to a local motel where she could study. Ember said, "I have a final tomorrow morning for a class towards my second master's degree. I am going to go to any hotel, cry for a little, and then study, as nothing will get in the way of me finishing my degree with honors." He looked at her, dumbfounded.

When she got to the motel, she studied a little but did not read much because her eyes were filled with tears all night. She ended up getting an "A" on her final and moving out into her first apartment the following week by using a cash advance on her credit card.

When her dad found out about her arrest, he blamed Ember, telling her he knew she would get arrested for something. He said she should have been out on her own a long time ago and this would have never happened. When he found out where Ember was living after she was arrested, he said she chose to live in a "run down building with the rest of the losers in the world" and that she would never amount to anything. To her dad, it may not have been nice, but to her, it was a place of her own where she hoped to find peace from the chaos, and she cherished it and was thankful for it.

As time went on, Ember's dad insisted she help finance a car for him since he had purchased her first car for her (the same one he took back). He asked Ember if she had enough credit to do this for him. Ember was embarrassed to tell him how much credit she had outstanding because she always wanted him to think she could do everything on her own, so she initially told him she did have the credit. When it came down to going to buy the car for him, Ember decided she was going to admit that she was overextended on credit and could not help him. When Ember told her dad how much money she owed, he became angry and told her that she was a liar and that she should never have told him she could buy a car for him. So, he offered to give her financial advice for a $100 fee. He told Ember that she was in danger and that he would figure out a way for her to pay off her bills faster if she gave him $100 immediately. Again, he was kicking her when she was already down. Ember was telling him she was broke, and he was using the situation to make a profit for himself. All Ember could think was, "What an asshole! He always told me I should respect my father but what if my father has no respect for me?"

Her dad ended up offering to pay her some money back. He began making the minimum payment on one of her credit cards for a little while. One day, her sister got drunk and totaled their mom's car in the middle of the night. She drove the car home with the airbags deployed and went to sleep. No one knew what had occurred until the cops knocked at the door. She left the license plate on the pole she hit. She received tickets and had to appear in court. Their mom was fed up with her drinking, so she sent her to a treatment program. When their dad found out about what happened, he blamed Ember and their mom for giving Ember's sister money and "making her an alcoholic." Maybe he felt guilty for his absence or maybe it was another attempt at triangulation. Whatever his motive, he sent Ember's sister a $500 check with a card saying, "We all make mistakes." This money and card for her sister came in the mail just a week after he called Ember and asked her why the balance on the credit card was still so high. Ember explained that the interest rate was high, and he was only making minimum payments. This barely made a dent in the amount owed. He disputed the fact that he still owed her the money. He started out saying he would pay her $300 a week, then $100, and then he said he didn't remember owing her that amount at all. That was only one credit card. What about the rest of the money she had lent him that was still unpaid? They argued and soon began to speak less.

He suggested that they go to counseling since they could not get along. Ember agreed to go, hoping that some issues would be resolved. When they got to the counselor, her father's wife at the time took a piece of paper from the bulletin board and asked the receptionist to make three copies of it. Then, she handed Ember and her dad a copy. She laughed as she read the rules of counseling, especially the one that read, "No punching or hitting." Ember was glad she found it funny because Ember sure didn't. What Ember found funny was how his wife had no idea she would be used for all her money and would be crying and in debt by the end of their marriage. But people must learn for themselves sometimes, just as Ember had to. Ember should've known that the reason her dad wanted to go to counseling was to talk about how upset he was that he had to pay Ember the money back on the credit card. That was all they discussed. How he felt Ember should respect him and not make him pay, as he was sick and unable to. Again, Ember had gotten her hopes up high and wished he was going to counseling to change. But he wasn't ready. She thought, "Who knows if he will ever be ready?" It was just another pathetic attempt for him to use Ember and make her feel like shit. So, she told him to just forget about paying her but to never call her again for anything.

When Ember saw her sister open that card with the check inside, it felt like a knife went through Ember's heart. She was so hurt. Her sister even knew it was wrong and offered to give the check to her. That wouldn't make it right, nor would it have made Ember feel better. The point was how could her dad be that cold?

Ember's sister was a baby when their parents got divorced. Her sister began ignoring their father and refused to have a relationship with him at an early age. This only made him try harder to make her love him. He would chase her, write her letters, and send her money, and she still didn't give him the time of day. On the other hand, he treated Ember, the daughter who was always there for him, like she didn't matter at all. Ember would do everything she could to make him love her, but it wasn't good enough. That was also how Ember would be with most of the men who entered her life. Ember learned the hard way that setting boundaries and cutting toxicity out of your life sometimes makes people like you more while going out of your way for toxic people will only make them try to use you even more and disrespect you. Her dad viewed her sister as the stronger daughter, the one who stood up for herself. He viewed Ember as the weak one, the one he could take advantage of.

Ember hated the fact that she still had to work two jobs and struggle and be tired of trying to do what she thought was help. But she dealt with it. Her mom thought she was a shopaholic because it was the only explanation she could come up with as to why Ember was in so much debt. Ember wouldn't dare tell her that she gave her dad all that money because her mother would be furious and would say, "I told you so." So, Ember told her mother that she incurred the debt herself. The truth is that some of the bills were her own. Ember felt so ugly and worthless that she began buying clothes and shoes and getting her hair and nails done so that she could look good on the outside and cover up what she was feeling on the inside. All the shopping didn't work, though. The pain was still embedded in her. She learned that, unless she dealt with it head-on, it would never go away. So, she dealt with it. She worked every day and tried her best to keep her head up and to keep a smile on her pretty face.

When her dad married his third wife, he told her that she was just jealous because he was married three times and Ember couldn't even get married once at age 29. When he was saying this and other hurtful things, they were walking near a lake and a grassy area in his neighborhood. In the middle of the conversation, he swatted a fly and said, "These flies must be here because of the water." Ember replied, "They will be here as long as you are here." Her dad looked puzzled and said, "What do you mean?" She answered, "The flies are here because I am walking with a piece of shit." She ran to her car and cried hysterically as she drove home that day.

It was that day Ember realized he didn't care about whether she was arrested, dead, homeless, sad, hurt, or upset. It didn't matter. All that ever mattered to her father was how much money he could get from her. So, she decided at that moment that she was going to stop giving him money and stop putting up with all his abuse. And she did. For a while, not talking to him hurt because she wanted to have a healthy relationship with him so badly. Ember also was worried about him, but she had to cut him off. This also made her realize that not only was he not getting any more money from her, but she would also not support anyone else. It was time to concentrate on herself, which is what she should have been doing all along. But she still had to clean up the years of enabling and spending. Her dad's ex-wives and girlfriends were not so lucky. Each one of them went bankrupt and ended up owing hundreds of thousands of dollars to creditors.

One day, while she was not on speaking terms with her father, Ember had a conversation with a co-worker. He said, "It is worse to give too much than to take too much because when you give, you are enabling bad behavior." Ember said, "You are so right about that! I am going to use that quote, if you don't mind." He answered, "Sure, I will send you the bill in the mail for the counseling session." She said, "You can send it, but I can't afford to pay it because I am one who gave too much throughout my life and now, I am broke." They both laughed but Ember was crying inside.

CHAPTER THREE

"Just Perfect" Joseph

Many of the characteristics that Ember displayed as a child and adolescent spilled over into her teenage years and would also later spill over into her relationships with men. This is why she truly began to believe that the past molds who a person becomes. When she was in eighth grade, her sister was in second grade. Ember would always wait near the flagpole after school so that they could walk home together. Ember's sister had a friend in her class named Ann. Ann's cousin, Joseph, would always pick Ann up from school. He was in high school but would come to walk Ann home every day. Ember's sister and her friend would always try to get Ember and Joseph to walk together. Eventually, they would all walk the same way home together. They talked and laughed but Ember didn't think anything of it.

One day, her sister told her that she had a phone call. When Ember picked it up, to her surprise, it was Joseph. He asked if they could hang out one day when he brings Ann over to play with her sister. Ember told him that she would love to hang out with him. When she hung up,

Ember was so excited and nervous at the same time. She thought, "What would we do when he comes over? What should I wear? How should I act? What if he doesn't like me after we hang out?"

They ended up hanging out and all her fears were put to rest. They both had a lot in common. He liked basketball and so did Ember, so they decided to play one on one in her backyard. It was the end of spring and Ember began to feel that it was going to be a great summer. The two hung out very often throughout the whole summer. They went to the town pool, watched movies, and continued to play basketball.

One day, Ember was walking Joseph through the alleyway of her house when he pinned her against the wall and kissed her. It was the first time she had ever kissed anyone. As soon as he left, Ember went inside and brushed her teeth and tongue. EWWW! She liked him but it felt weird to have someone else's tongue in her mouth.

The next week, her mom (who liked Joseph a lot and approved of them hanging out), invited Joseph to the beach with them. They swam all day, took pictures together, and had tons of fun. He told Ember to run on the beach and he would tackle her. She began running and he tackled her. He lay near her in the sand and asked her if she wanted to be his girlfriend. Ember was at a loss for words. She couldn't believe it. He liked her. She was so happy and told him that she would love to be his girl. He kissed her and made her feel so happy and safe inside.

They hung out for the rest of the summer. Before Ember knew it, it was a year later, and they were still going out and happy as could be. One night, he came over and said that he had to move far away because his family was moving. Ember was crushed. She thought, "How would we see each other now? He would have to take two busses and a train to see me." Ember talked to her mom about it, and she said that she would let him sleep over on the weekends to make it easier for them to see each other. He was willing to get to Ember no matter what it took.

That summer, they would still play basketball together. Her basketball hoop was right over the stairway to the basement. Every time the ball would go down the stairs to the basement, they would go and get it together. He would touch and kiss her, and she would get butterflies in her stomach. She began to really fall in love with Joseph.

When he wasn't around, Ember would put her hand on her head and say to her mom or her sister, "Joseph loves me." They would laugh and were happy for Ember. Her mother said that he was a good kid, and her sister was happy that she hooked them up with the help of Ann. He had once done a project for school and included Ember in it. At the end of the paper was a picture of them and he wrote that he planned to be a doctor, marry Ember, and live in a house with a heart- shaped pool. What more could she ever ask for?

One day, they went into the basement and things got serious. He began fingering Ember, and she began jerking him off. He came on her and she did not know what happened. She had never experienced anything like this before. Was it normal? What comes next? Ember had no idea. All she knew was that she loved Joseph and wanted to be happy with him for the rest of her life.

After a while, Joseph asked Ember when they were going to have sex. He was a virgin and so was Ember. She was scared. She did not want to get pregnant or get a disease but was afraid to talk to him about it. He told Ember that he loved her, that he cherished their time together, and that he would wait if he had to because she was special.

He did wait until she was ready, which was two years later. When he slept over, Ember would sleep in her bedroom, and he slept on the couch in the living room. They planned for him to go into Ember's room when everyone was sleeping one night. He went in and she told him she was ready. She asked him to make sure he had a condom. He said that he wanted to be safe, and did have a condom.

They had sex that night. After they did it, he hugged her, kissed her, and told her that he loved her dearly. Ember felt so good. Before the sun came up, she asked him to take the condom and throw it down the sewer of her block so no one would find it. He got up and told her that he did.

They woke up the next day to Ember's mom screaming. She sat the two of them down and told them that she found a condom in the kitchen garbage can. She was upset and told them that Joseph could not sleep over anymore. She said that she did not want them having sex in her house. She said that Ember could get pregnant, and she did not want that to happen. Ember was mad at Joseph because he said that he was careful when he threw the condom out. Before he left that day, he told Ember that he did throw the condom out in the sewer and that he did not know how her mom knew about them having sex. Now, Ember was even angrier because he lied to her. She told him to leave because she needed time alone.

When he left, Ember talked to her mom again. She kept asking Ember if the condom was on the whole time. Ember began thinking and becoming nervous that she could be pregnant. Her mother called the doctor and had the morning-after pill prescribed for her just in case. She was furious and Ember was embarrassed. What seemed so right went so wrong in the blink of an eye.

Her mom told her that she was wrong about Joseph, and she said that he was not welcome in her house anymore. Joseph told Ember that he still loved her and that he would continue to do whatever it took to see her.

CHAPTER FOUR

Notorious Nate

Ember was working at a pizzeria and going to school. Every chance she would get, she would hang out with Joseph. There was a guy who would always walk past the pizzeria and stare at Ember. One night, as she was walking home from work, this guy stopped her and introduced himself. He said his name was Nate. She told him that it was nice to meet him but that she had a boyfriend. He was not that cute to her, but he was interested in her.

One night, Ember's friend, Sophie, picked her up from work. As they were walking home, they saw Nate and his friend. He came up to them and said hello. They wanted to hang out with Ember and Sophie. Ember told Sophie that she did not think that he was cute and that she loved Joseph. Sophie told Ember that she thought Nate was very cute and that they should hang out with them because Sophie thought his friend was cute too.

They ended up hanging out that night. Nate told Ember that he liked her from the first day that he saw her. He said that he thought she was beautiful and that he wanted to have another chance to see her again. They exchanged phone numbers, but Ember made it clear that they were only going to be friends.

Nate was very different from Joseph. He was more of a thug. Joseph was clean-cut, had a job, and had goals in life. Nate did not work, dressed in baggy jeans and long t-shirts, and used slang words. But there was something about Nate that Ember found appealing. Maybe it was that he was rugged. He was exciting to be around. He was older than her and she liked the way he talked. She figured she would keep him around as a friend.

Nate and Ember began hanging out more and more. One night, they hung out and he was drunk. He told her that he liked her, and he kissed her. She never imagined that she would ever kiss anyone other than Joseph. She felt bad that it happened because Joseph was the one she loved. Ember figured she would have to wait and see what would happen.

Joseph eventually bought a car at an auction for $500 so that he could come see Ember more often. The passenger side door didn't open so she would have to go in through the trunk. When she told her dad about it, she was happy. Her dad told her that he was a loser because he should be able to buy a better car than that to take her out if she was going to be his girl. Ember was mad at her dad for saying that but was used to it by then. Whenever she was proud or happy about something, her dad always had a way to ruin her happiness by saying something negative.

She was not ready to let go of Joseph despite how hard it was for them to see each other but she also wanted to continue seeing Nate as well. One day, Nate and Ember were walking down the block when he grabbed her hand. As they turned the corner, they saw Joseph's best friend. His expression said it all. Ember knew she was in trouble. She had a huge knot in her stomach. How was she going to explain this?

Joseph called her screaming and yelling. He was upset at what his friend had told him. Ember tried to calm him down and told him that she and Nate were only friends, but he didn't seem to believe it. Joseph came rushing down to see Ember and they discussed it. Ember reassured him that nothing was going on and that she only wanted to be with him.

Little did Ember know that Joseph had found Nate's number and had called him without her knowing. He asked Nate to invite Ember over to his house and Joseph planned to be there to catch her. Nate, however, liked Ember and told her about the plan. Nate also told Ember that Joseph asked him if they "went all the way." Nate told Ember he told Joseph that they had not.

Later, she would find that Nate did tell Joseph they had sex even though they didn't. It was too late-Joseph was already gone. Nate's plan of breaking them up had succeeded. Ember was upset that she had hurt Joseph and that he did not want to have anything to do with her. At the same time, she was also excited to find out what would happen next with Nate.

Nate and Ember eventually started seeing each other every day. Although he never had any money to take her out, he would pick her up and they would go to the park or just hang out around the neighborhood. She met most of his friends and he met most of hers. One day, she called him, and his mother answered. She asked Ember who was calling. Ember responded by saying that she was his friend. His mother said if Ember was his friend, she would leave him alone because he was always getting into trouble because of his friends. Ember didn't understand what she meant but also did not bother to ask him the next time he called. She liked Nate and wanted to be with him no matter what.

One thing about Nate was that he would always be jealous and accuse her of cheating on him, although she never did. She would soon find out that he was blaming her, but he was the one cheating. Ember made Nate wait a year before she had sex with him. She knew he was experienced, and she only had sex with one person. She told Nate she was a virgin since she had only had sex one time before with Joseph. It was great that he was willing to wait. Ember thought it meant he loved her.

The first summer they were together, she went on her usual annual family vacation with her mom and her sister. When Ember returned, Nate did not make much effort to see her. She happened to go to a fast-food restaurant in her neighborhood one day when she came back and she saw him there. He had a big hickey on his neck. His friend was with him. When Ember asked him who the hickey was from, he said it wasn't a hickey and that his friend, who also agreed, had scratched him while playing basketball. Ember didn't believe that deep down inside, but she stayed with him only to find out a few months later that her gut feeling was right. He had sex with a girl from their neighborhood while Ember was away. She was one of Ember's friend's friends. Ember began to hate her. She confronted her and the girl admitted it, adding that it meant nothing to her because they were both drunk and she didn't enjoy it. It meant something to Ember. She was heartbroken. She still hadn't had sex with him and now she realized that the only reason he was waiting was because he was having sex with someone else.

The relationship started off rocky, but he apologized. He told Ember he loved her and that he had made a terrible mistake. Nate cried and said he didn't want to lose Ember. She loved him so she forgave him. So, they continued to see each other. Ember told him that if he really liked her, he would have to wait longer to have sex. He said that he would wait until she was ready and felt comfortable because she was worth it. So, they continued to hang out and have fun.

One day, about a year after they started dating, he came through the alleyway, jumped up to the second floor, and tapped Ember's bedroom window at about 2 am. She opened the window and was surprised to see him there. She snuck him into her bedroom, and they had sex. She kept telling him that they had to use a condom because she did not want to get pregnant or get a disease. He said he did not have a disease, and he would pull out. Ember was scared to death but still let him have sex with her.

To Ember's surprise, he had the smallest penis any man could ever have! She felt as though she was having sex with another girl. She did not feel anything at all. He came in less than a minute and he pulled out like he said he would. Ember lay down and thought, "That's it? Is that what all the hype is about? Now I know why the girl he cheated on me with said she didn't enjoy it. Neither did I and I was sober."

As they were lying down after having sex, he started telling her about the first time he had sex, as she made him believe it was the first time she ever had sex. He said it was with a girl named Trinisha who he barely knew. His boys were "running train" on her. As one guy left the room, another guy would go in. He said he was the second one that night to have sex with her. Ember immediately got sick to her stomach and could not believe what she was hearing. "He couldn't tell me this before we had sex, or better yet-not tell me at all?" How dare he talk about this right after I gave myself to him? And he has the nerve to tell me he doesn't have a disease?" Ember was scared but did not know how to handle it. Now she had to worry about diseases on top of getting pregnant and ruining her life. He went on to tell her that those days were over because he loved her. He said that having sex with Ember was different than having sex with anyone else. He said it was a completely different feeling because he loved her.

Ember hadn't seen her father in a while and this male attention and "love" from Nate felt so good that she erased what he had told her about his first sexual experience out of her mind. Nate and Ember continued having sex late at night. He would knock on her window and Ember would let him in. It only worked out because her mom's room was on the other side of the house. Ember would listen near the wall and, when she heard her mom snoring, she knew it was okay for him to come in.

Sometimes, he would climb through the window with a chair from the backyard, as they did not want her mom to wake up from the back door alarm. Ember thought it was like something out of a fairytale. Little did she know it was going to turn out to be like something out of a horror movie.

She couldn't remember the first time it happened, but it happened. Nate hit Ember. He didn't only hit her once. Every time he would hit her, he would start out by calling her names. He would say how he was the best thing that could happen to her, and she could never find anyone like him or anyone who would want her. He would call her names for no reason. He would call her ugly and scream it while they were walking outside so others could hear. He would completely humiliate Ember and make her want to stay inside and hide. There were many occasions when he would raise his fist to act like he was going to hit her and then laugh when she would duck and get scared. It seemed to amuse him.

One weekend, Ember's mom went on vacation and her sister and Ember were home with their grandma. Nate and his friends came over and Ember was with her friend, Sophie. Sophie liked one of Nate's friends. Nate thought it was Ember who liked his friend. Nate did his usual name-calling, called Ember a slut, and pushed her. He pushed her so hard that she fell on the ground and hurt her arm. The bone in her elbow popped out, causing her a lot of pain. Sophie yelled at Nate and then took Ember inside. Ember lay down and cried. She was hurt and embarrassed. She also thought she would lose Nate forever. When he came inside to see if Ember was okay, she felt relieved. She told him to leave. She didn't want to look like a fool for still talking to him after what he did.

The next day, Ember went to the emergency room on a bus with Sophie and her sister. On the way, he got on the same bus and became angry because she had ignored him. He began to make a scene on the bus. He said he was going to his friend Diana's house to get over it. Ember wondered how he could go to hang out with another girl when he just hurt her and claimed to love her. Ember got mad and started to yell at him. He grabbed her bus money right out of her hand. Ember, her sister, and Sophie had to walk home from the emergency room because they had no bus fare. To make it even worse, Ember had a broken arm, and her baby sister had to witness all of this. She felt like a failure. When was enough going to be enough?

There was a time when Nate broke his leg and needed crutches to walk. Ember and Nate had an argument, and he got out of the car and broke her mom's car windshield with one of his crutches and hit her in the face with it. One other time, when he became jealous of her neighbor, he hit her and called her horrible names in front of her little sister, terrifying her. Ember was particularly upset about this time because she never wanted her sister to witness this. She didn't want her to grow up thinking it was okay to be treated like that. Ember still thought it was okay for her to be hit because she had no self-confidence. It was shredded to pieces.

One day, Nate had something that looked like white powder in his nose when he went to see Ember. When she questioned it, he said, "How dare you ask me if I do drugs? My dad used to use drugs and hit my mom when I was little. I would never do drugs." Ember felt so bad for questioning him after that. Then she thought to herself, "You witnessed your dad hit your mom and that didn't stop you from hitting me. What makes me think you witnessing your dad do drugs would make you not do drugs?" But Ember let it go to avoid any more problems.

Another time, Ember showed up at one of Nate's friend's houses because she suspected he was sleeping over and cheating on her. When she got there, he answered the door in his boxers. She got so upset that she slapped him across the face. He threw Ember down the front stairs and kicked her in the face with his boot. He then pulled her hair and spit on her. Ember was screaming and crying. His friend came outside and told her to stop making noise in her neighborhood. Ember ended up in the hospital that night alone while he went back inside and continued whatever it was that he was doing.

Another day, Ember snuck Nate in when her mom wasn't home. They were hanging out and she realized her mom came home early. Her mother was at the front door and her mother's friend was at the back door, probably because they suspected Ember had Nate over. They were caught. That night, Ember's mom said her gold cross that her father gave her before he died was missing. Ember was so mad at her when she blamed Nate for taking it. He would never do that. Maybe she misplaced it. Ember would later find out that maybe she was wrong.

When her mom found out about Nate abusing her, she made Ember file a restraining order. She didn't want to do it, but her mother said she would kick her out if she didn't. So, she did. After her mother later found her in her room with Nate and kicked her out, Ember dropped the restraining order. She justified it by blaming her mom for kicking her out. She didn't think it was that serious. She couldn't see what harm Nate was causing her. When Ember told her dad that she was filing a restraining order against Nate, instead of being happy, he said she was ruining Nate's life, and she should "leave that poor man alone." Talk about blaming the victim.

No one can completely understand domestic violence until they have been through it. Yes, Ember was the girl who wouldn't leave no matter what. She wanted him to know she was a loyal girlfriend and would do anything not to lose him. People, including her mom and family, thought she was crazy. They would ask why she wouldn't just leave him. Maybe it was because she began to believe she wasn't good enough. She began to believe that no one else would ever love her. Why wouldn't she believe that? Her own father didn't even love her.

One night, Ember's mom stopped snoring when Nate was in her room. Ember heard her get up from her bed. Ember got nervous and told Nate to hide in the closet. He said he didn't want to. As she pushed him into the closet, her mom came in and caught them. He was in his boxers. As her mom began screaming, he pushed her out of the way and ran outside. Ember knew she was in trouble. This was not the first time her mom got mad at her for being with him. He had been over when her mom was at work and had broken several of her cell phones and beepers when accusing Ember of cheating on him. He would make her ninety-year-old grandmother nervous, causing her to tell her mom what went on when she came home from work. But this was the last time. Ember's mom called Nate's mom and said, "Your son was in my house without my permission." His mother replied, "If my son was in your house, it is because your daughter let him in." Ember's mom was furious. That was the day Ember became homeless, as her mother kicked her out.

Ember had no choice but to live with Nate and his mother. This was at a crucial time in her life. She had just graduated high school and got accepted into college. She had exceptional grades and could attend any school she wanted to. She didn't put much thought into it and just decided to attend the first school that accepted her. Her mom wanted Ember to dorm at the college so she could have a complete college experience, hoping Ember would leave Nate for good. Ember was contemplating whether she should go to a dorm. It was the summer before her first year of college, so she continued to work two jobs until she came to a decision. Ember grew up fast. She always worked two jobs to help support her father's gambling addiction, to pay for the things she needed, and to buy nice things for her sister, mom, and Nate. You would think Nate would work at least one job to help them out, especially after he saw Ember's struggle and made it harder. But he didn't even try to look for a job and always made excuses as to why he couldn't get a job.

Ember's dad bought her a car when she graduated high school. Ember was mad when her mom advised her not to get too attached to the car, as her dad would eventually take it back like he did with everything else. He would buy Ember things to prove he was a good father when he was winning at gambling and would take them back when he would lose and realized he could not afford them. And Ember was like a puppet, getting her hopes up high and believing that this was her car. Her father made a rule and said no one was allowed in the car except Ember because his wife at the time was paying for the insurance and it was in her name. What kind of rule is that for a teenager who just got a new car? Ember immediately broke the rule, not thinking it was that serious.

One day, when Ember was on her way to one of her jobs, she realized her car was not where she had parked it the night before. Ember panicked and called her dad, as she thought someone had stolen it. She should've known better. Her dad came and took it away because he said she had people in it and was not following the rules. Her mom was right. He did this to Ember at a time when she needed the car more than ever. She was practically homeless and working hard to try to make it. Now, she had to take two buses to get to work and even more to make it to her second job. But she knew she wouldn't quit or drop out of school. She always had this drive inside of her to make it and to prove to everyone, including herself, that she could do it even if the odds were against her. Ember became very sick at the time because Nate refused to turn off the fan at night and she got a bad cold with a fever. But she pressed on and went to work. She had no other choice.

Ember's mom wrote her a letter shortly after she kicked out of the house saying that she knew Ember was going to end up "pregnant and drug addicted" and she didn't want her back in the house. It hurt but Ember would prove them wrong about everything. Everything except the fact that Nate was right for her and that he was a good man. After years of heartache, Ember would realize he wasn't. But she had to learn and go through it on her own.

One day, as Ember was getting ready for work, she came across a piece of paper that read, "Girls that I played her out with" followed by a list of girls' names. Ember was so hurt. When she confronted Nate, he became angry and said he only wrote that to get her mad because he knew she would find it. Ember would later find out that the list was all true, plus some. But she decided to believe him again because she was in denial and had nowhere to go and no one else to care for her and love her.

One night, there was a knock at Nate's door. It was Ember's dad and his girlfriend at the time. Her dad told her that she was in danger and could go live with him. Ember didn't want to, but he told her that she could still see Nate and would have a greater opportunity to better herself if she were living with him. Ember went with her dad. That was probably the biggest mistake of her life.

Ember's dad made her forge her mom's name in the beginning of her first year at college so she didn't have to dorm and so the money her mom paid could go to him. He said Ember had to do this if she wanted to stay with him. He contacted the school and told them that Ember's mom was crazy, threw Ember out, and stole her money when he was the one who was using Ember for money to support his gambling addiction. Her dad made her work two jobs and pay rent while going to school. She was miserable. He had her open credit cards, saying she had to buy things that she needed but actually made her use the credit for him. He was evil to her, but she had to deal with it while her stepsister had her mom paying for everything. Her step-sister had a brand-new car, new clothes, and a boyfriend who bought her nice things and treated her like a princess. Ember's dad even took money from her one Christmas and bought her sister a gift with HER money. This made her feel worse than shit. Ember would ask herself, "What did I do to deserve this?"

Ember kept seeing Nate. She would take buses to her old neighborhood, and they would hang out. One time, Nate picked her up in a jeep. She knew it couldn't be his. When she saw the screwdriver in the ignition, she realized it had been stolen. Ember got into it anyway. He had the jeep for about a month before he got caught and was arrested. Ember thought to herself, "I could have been arrested with him, which would have ruined my future. How stupid was I to ever get in that car?" She knew so many girls who got in trouble with the law because of their boyfriends and she didn't want to be one of them. She pawned all her jewelry and took out a cash advance on her credit card to bail him out. Nate's mom went with Ember and co-signed. This must have been what she was referring to the first time Ember spoke to her on the phone. When he was released, he went straight to his friend's house. When Ember called him and screamed at him, he said that Ember shouldn't have bailed him out, as he "didn't ask her to." He wasn't going to court, and he could care less about his mother and Ember. Ember was so afraid the bail bondsmen would come after her. And they did. She turned him in. She had to wait until the whole process was over until she was no longer responsible for him getting to court. Ember learned her lesson quickly. She would never bail anyone out ever again no matter what. She would never sign her name for anyone either.

Still, though, she stayed with him. When she would harass him about cheating on her, he would get mad, and they would argue. He began hanging out with a girl and her husband, both of whom Ember didn't know. Nate said he never introduced Ember because Ember didn't smoke weed or drink and that is what he did there. Ember decided she had to start smoking weed to fit in and be a part of his circle of friends. So, she had her best friend teach her how to. She bought a bag of weed from her friend and brought it with her the next time that she went to see Nate. She told him they were going to smoke together and showed him the weed. Nate then introduced her to his friends. She was glad to learn that the girl, Rosa, was about 400 pounds and had a husband anyway. Now Ember didn't have to wonder if he was cheating while he went over there. She ended up smoking weed that one time and hated it. She didn't usually allow herself to be peer pressured, but she did it to further investigate her suspicions. She never did it again despite Nate asking her to. She wanted to prove her mom wrong. She would never be a drug addict like her mother wrote in that letter. Little did Ember know she would be addicted to toxicity and abuse most of her life, though.

Ember's mom decided to sell her house and move to a new neighborhood after about a year of Ember attending college. Ember decided to transfer to a new school in New York where she could have a fresh start. Her mom told her that she could live with her, her sister, and her grandmother in the new house if Nate did not know where they lived. She offered this after the damage was done, though.

Ember went back to live with her mom in the old house for a little while until they were ready to move to the new house. One of the conditions of living with her mom again was that she had to get a restraining order against Nate because her mom did not want him near her house. Ember was planning on not seeing Nate again and trying to get over him and move on with her life. She had had enough of being abused both physically and emotionally. She ignored his calls and didn't plan to see him. She wanted to start a new life. She wanted to start fresh. It was flattering that he called her and left messages about how much he loved and missed her, but she also thought about how abusive he was and how he could ruin her future, so she continued to ignore him.

Ember was in her mother's car driving to New York to give a presentation for her public speaking class at her new college. She was excited because school was the one opportunity she had to feel good about herself. As she was driving, suddenly, a car stopped short in front of her and a guy began running to her car door and pulled her out of the car. It all happened so fast. It was Nate. He was driving someone's car. He pulled Ember's hair and began fighting her because he was mad that she had been ignoring him. A police officer happened to be passing by and witnessed this. He made Nate sit in his car and Ember sat in hers. Then, he came to Ember and said, "How do you know Jimmy?" She said, "Who? His name isn't Jimmy." The officer said, "His name isn't Jimmy?" She said, "No, it isn't. He is lying, probably because I have a restraining order against him." Ember gave the officer his real name and he was arrested. She begged the officer to let her go to school and he said this was serious and she had to go to the police department.

At the police department, the officer explained how he took domestic violence very seriously, as his mother was killed by her boyfriend. All she could think about was how Nate stopped her from giving her speech at school that she was so excited about. Ember completed all the paperwork and agreed to press charges. Nate was charged with seven different things, one being carjacking. It was then that Ember realized the officer wasn't playing. The cop told her that Nate was in the back "crying crocodile tears." Ember began to feel sorry for him. The officer called Ember's mom at work and told her what happened. She was upset but happy that Ember was okay and that she agreed to press charges.

Shortly after that day, Nate convinced her to be with him again. She wasn't ready to end it just yet. He told her that he loved her and hated to be without her. He told her he was scared to go to jail and would never hurt her again. Of course, she believed it. So, she went in front of a Grand Jury and had the charges against him dropped. She stayed with him.

Just before they moved, Ember received a phone call from a girl asking for a person named Rose. Ember told the girl that she had the wrong number, and then the girl asked Ember for her name. When Ember told the girl her name, the girl told Ember that she was Nate's friend's girlfriend, her name was Angela, and that she knew Ember was dating Nate. She said that Nate, her, and her boyfriend were at a girl named Rose's house one day, and all of them were sniffing heroin. She said Nate and her boyfriend had sex with Rose in front of her and that Rose tried to rape her. Ember couldn't believe what she was hearing.

She told Ember that she got her number from her boyfriend's phone and thought Ember was Rose. Ember and Angela planned to meet each other and follow Nate and her boyfriend. Ember had to find out if her story had any truth to it. Angela said she knew where they hung out. They were always at Nate's friend Peter's house. They went there and found Nate outside. He was surprised to see them. Ember's heart was racing, almost beating out of her chest. Before Ember could confront him, Nate asked Ember and Angela if they wanted to go upstairs, and they did. When they got upstairs, there were eight girls, who were much older than Ember, with Nate, Angela's boyfriend, and Peter. He said Ember could check on him any time she wanted to because he was only hanging out. Ember played it cool and told him she was leaving after only a few minutes.

It was a bad neighborhood. When he walked her downstairs, a girl mumbled, "Fuck you, bitch." Ember ignored it. Then, she came up to Ember outside and said, "Bitch, I'm talking to you," and pushed her. Ember shoved her back, and they started to fight. Suddenly, seven other girls and two men jumped in. They pushed Ember to the ground. Ember concentrated on one girl, pulled out her weave, and kicked everyone as she fell to the ground. When she was finally able to get up, she was pinned up against a wall. There was a beer bottle on the ledge when she got up, so she grabbed it, and everyone moved back. As Ember picked it up, a little bit of beer splashed one of the girls in the face, and round two began. They followed her as she ran to her car. The whole time, Ember was screaming and telling Nate and Angela's boyfriend to call the police or to do something to help her. She made it to her car alive and okay, although she was now barefoot, and her clothes were ripped. She just couldn't understand why Nate didn't jump in to protect her. They are right when they say a coward abuses his girl but is never brave enough to fight anyone else. When she needed him the most during a fight she would never have been in if it weren't for him, he wasn't there. To make matters worse, Ember left by herself while Nate stayed to continue with his get-together.

Angela later told her that her boyfriend would not let her help her or call the police. The next day, Angela told Ember that Nate and her boyfriend would be back at Rose's house. Ember was reluctant to go after all that happened. She had so much anger inside of her. Some of it was towards Nate, some towards Rose, and the rest toward herself for allowing all of this to happen. Ember decided she would go to her house to fight. So, that is just what she did. She went to Rose's house that night. They knocked and, when Rose asked who it was, she would not open the door when they told her. Ember began kicking her door until she opened it. Rose hid behind her couch as Ember confronted her. She said Ember was crazy, as Nate had told her, and that someone should call Angela's mother. Ember told her someone should call her mother, the police, or child protective services on her since she was doing all of this with her child there. Her husband stayed in another room. He must have been afraid and too ashamed to show his face. He yelled out that he was going to call the police. Ember screamed back and said someone should call the police on them for trying to rape Angela, and for drug use and prostitution, as Angela also told her that Nate and her boyfriend would pimp Rose out at a nearby hooker hotel. Ember was afraid she would lose her fist in Rose's fat when she punched her. Nate tried to break this fight up but was unsuccessful. It wasn't a fight. Ember punched her in the face once and then realized where she was. She was in her house, and it wasn't worth getting arrested over. So, Ember left. As she walked outside, she looked at Nate and said, "Congrats! At least now you can say you slept with four girls at one time since the bitch is 400 pounds." As she drove up the block, she could see red and blue lights from cop cars speeding towards the house. She saw her freedom flash in front of her. However, she never got arrested or even questioned. She left just in time.

When she got home, she told her mom she wanted to call the police and child protective services to get back at them. She felt like fighting the world; she couldn't deal with the pain. Her mom looked at her and said, "Don't worry. You don't have to do anything to get back at them. They will get what they deserve. Ignoring Nate and not talking to him will be the greatest revenge." Ember never forgot those words. She was teaching her acceptance, which she had a hard time with. She was right, Nate would eventually get his karma; all of them would (although Ember did not believe it at the time).

Even though this happened many years ago, Ember remembers it like it was yesterday. It was a Saturday night when she confronted Rose. She had a stomachache and felt sick until she could get to the doctor on Monday to be tested for sexually transmitted diseases. She was scared for her health and life. She was so afraid. She risked her life, her freedom, and her well-being just for choosing to stay with Nate while he was having sex with just about everyone behind her back. By some miracle, all her tests were negative. This chapter of her life was finally over for good. Now, she could work on picking up the pieces.

CHAPTER FIVE

Horrible Hector

Ember was hanging out with her friend, Sophie, and they drove by a liquor store where some guys were standing out front. Sophie knew one of the guys, so they began talking to him. His friend, Hector, came to the car and started flirting with Ember. She didn't think he was cute, but she was single and decided to give him her number when he asked for it.

A few days after they met, all of them decided to go to a park near the George Washington Bridge to hang out. Hector was there. He was a lot shorter than Ember, so he stood on a rock, and they began to kiss. After that night, Ember started to like him. He was cool to be around, and he would do silly things to make her laugh (sometimes, she couldn't figure out if he would do things and not realize they were stupid or if he was just not too smart and thought the things he did were normal). After a while, Hector became Ember's man. She lived with her mom, and he lived with his aunt, as his mother died when he was five years old. When Ember told Sophie that Hector was her boyfriend, she thought Ember was kidding. She couldn't believe Ember would ever entertain someone like him. Ember thought there was something cute about him, even though he was nowhere near her level. He had no education, no car, no aspirations, and was super short. Ember was used to accepting the bare minimum. So, she was content with having someone who could make her laugh and was nice to her. Little did she know that would quickly change, and the laughter would soon turn into a river of tears.

Ember received a call from the county jail one day. It was Nate. He was locked up. She accepted the call, and he told her how much he loved her and wanted her to visit. Ember decided to visit him. She got dressed up nicely and made sure to look her best. When she saw him, he greeted her with a huge smile. He started telling her how much he loved and missed her. He told her how happy he was that she wanted to work things out with him. Ember let him say everything he had to say. Then, she broke the news to him. She told him she was in love with someone else. She let him know that one of his friends saw her with her new man, just in case he didn't believe her. She told him she never wanted to see him again. As he put his hand up on the glass, a tear ran down his cheek. Ember got up, put the phone down, and walked away. She didn't turn back. She knew it killed him. He had done the same thing to her in the past. Being home alone worrying about what or who he was doing was torture. She felt like a prisoner for so many years when he hit her and called her names. She finally felt free. That was her closure. That day, all the built-up hurt and pain inside of her because of Nate had disappeared. Ember was finally able to let go. She told him what she had to tell him, and he had no choice but to listen. She hurt him and now he had plenty of time to think about it. Now, Ember could move on with her life and her new relationship.

When Nate got released from jail, he lived with his mother who had just moved next door to Hector and his aunt. What are the chances? The first time Nate saw Ember with Hector and realized she wasn't playing; they ended up having a fistfight. After Hector beat his ass, Nate just had to deal with the fact that she was gone forever. Ember probably went out with Hector to get over Nate. Even after all he had done to her, she still felt like she loved him, but she knew she had to move on. So, Ember picked the first guy who came along. It is better to be alone than to be unhappy and there is no use rushing into something to just regret it in the end, right? Well, Ember hadn't learned that hard lesson yet.

Hector would tell everyone that his name was H-Demo and that he wanted to be a rapper. Everyone would make fun of him when he would try to rap. All his rap songs went like this: "Yo! Yo! It's H Demo." One thing about Hector was that he could care less about what anyone else thought or said. He would always be himself. He used to jump up and down with his legs open and tell Ember and her sister that was his cowboy dance. They would always have good laughs, whether they were laughing with him or at him.

Ember's grandmother on her father's side passed away when she was with Hector. She went to her grandmother's apartment to gather her things. Instead of being there for her and helping her, she noticed Hector was going through her grandmother's things. When she asked what he was doing, he said he was looking for money, adding, "She has to have some somewhere." How rude and fucked up was he? Anyway, any money her grandma may have had was stolen from her dad way before she passed away. He borrowed from her life insurance and never paid it back, causing her undue stress and worry. Ember used to feel so bad for her that she would help her make payments when she could so her grandmother wouldn't worry.

As time went on, Hector began leaving Ember at his aunt's house with his grandmother while he would go out and drink with his friends. He would lie to her about where he was. One night, he called Ember from jail. When she asked what happened, he said he was trying to break up a fight between two girls and one claimed that he hit her. Ember soon learned the real story. He was walking down the street drunk and saw a girl. He pushed her down near the stairs of a house and told her, "You know you want me." He grabbed her wrists and held her down. She was able to get away and call the police. Ember couldn't believe it! She was dating a rapist. When he found out that Ember knew what really happened, he admitted he had a problem with cocaine and alcohol and told her that he needed help. When his aunt found out, she decided to move to Florida and leave him behind. He ended up being homeless. As horrible as what he did was, she decided to stay with him because he admitted he had a problem and needed help, and she felt bad. Ember went to the shelter every day to see him and make sure he was ok. Ember eventually ended up giving him money to get on his feet and rent a room. He rented a room and worked at a temporary agency for minimum wage.

Hector decided to attend inpatient drug treatment during the holidays a year later. He had a pass to go home on Thanksgiving. Ember's mom let him come over to be with them since he didn't have any other family. Her mom also invited her dad over that year since he didn't have anywhere else to go either. At the end of the night, they drove Ember's dad home, and he asked, "What is that noise coming from the back seat?" Hector replied, "Oh, that is just me opening a Corona." As soon as they pulled up to her dad's apartment, her dad jumped out of the car. Hector reached over Ember's shoulder, beeped the horn, and screamed, "Hey, next time, I will bring the cocaine." Ember's dad walked into his apartment. That Thanksgiving, Ember was thankful that Hector did that. It showed her how her dad didn't have the balls to say or do anything. After all, Hector wasn't the only one who had an addiction. Just because her dad wasn't addicted to alcohol or drugs didn't mean he wasn't an addict. Gambling was just as bad or even worse. Hector admitted he had a problem whereas her dad always denied it. It also made her realize how she was attracted to addicts, probably because her dad was one. Would that ever change? When would she find someone to help her instead of her trying to help everyone else and feeling bad for those who made their own decisions?

That same day, Hector and Ember were having sex, and he pulled her birth control patch off her skin when she had just started it. He said she didn't need it. Then, he did not pull out. It was the first time anyone ever did this. Even though she had been in two previous relationships for years, she never had to worry because they either used a condom or they pulled out. She figured it would be ok. What would the chances be that she would get pregnant? She began feeling sick after that, but she figured it was just her being nervous. She missed her period and decided to take a pregnancy test. She was shaking while peeing on the stick. There were two lines. Ember was pregnant! At the time, she was 22 years old. She was going out with a person who could not support himself. Instead of saving money to move out on her own, all her money went to him and her dad. What was she going to do? She told her mom. Her mom said that if she decided to have the baby, she couldn't live with her. She went back and forth for weeks trying to decide what to do.

She had a job as an alcohol and drug counselor at the time. There was a client of hers who got pregnant by another client at the same time Ember was pregnant. The client was so happy during every session. She would talk about staying clean and being with the father of her child. The client spoke about how she and her boyfriend were going to be the best parents they could be. She had no idea Ember was pregnant because she didn't tell anyone. She figured if her client could have a baby while in treatment, why couldn't Ember have one too? She sought counseling on her own to figure it out.

In the meantime, Hector said that Ember being pregnant reminded him of his daughter and baby mother in Puerto Rico and how he was not there with them. Days later, after not hearing from him, Ember went by Hector's place and was told he left. She received a call later that day from him. Hector told her his cousin had paid for a one-way plane ticket, and he was in Puerto Rico. After all the contemplating Ember went through and the tears she cried, her decision on whether or not to keep the baby was made. She didn't want to bring a baby into the world without any support or without a father. Even though Ember had a father, he wasn't ever there for her, and she didn't want to make another person ever have to feel the way she did. Ember did not want the baby to suffer because she chose to have sex with a loser. She realized she should have thought of that before getting pregnant, but she didn't. So, she went through with the abortion. Ember was so sad. She felt horrible. And she dealt with all her feelings about it by herself. From that day on, she would cry every day on Mother's Day and every year around the time she had the abortion. For someone so smart with everything else, she was so stupid when it came to relationships.

To make matters worse, Hector called her from Puerto Rico a few months after she had the abortion and said he changed his mind and wanted to be a father again. It hurt her so badly. She did not have the heart to tell him she had an abortion, so she told him she lost the baby because she was stressed and upset. In that moment, she began to regret what she did. Little did Ember know that her decision would be more life-changing than she could ever imagine. She would never have another opportunity to have a child again. Hector not only took some of her youth but also took the opportunity to have a child away from her.

CHAPTER SIX

The Crooked O

After staying home and feeling sorry for herself about all she had been through with Hector, Ember went clubbing one night with a friend from high school. They had fun and danced all night even though they didn't meet anyone. As they drove out of the parking lot, these guys in a truck pulled up next to them. The driver asked them if they wanted to go for pancakes. They laughed and started talking to them. Ember exchanged numbers with the driver, Oscar. He was cute and he had a car (Well, she was hoping it was his). She hoped that he would call her. After three days, she was on her way to the gym when she received a call from a New York number she didn't know. She figured it was him! They talked and he asked her if she lived near the Garden State Plaza mall. Ember said she did, and they planned to meet there the following day.

They went to a department store when they met at the mall. Oscar picked up a $2,000 handbag and said, "This would be a great birthday gift if I were in a relationship." After the mall, they went out to eat.

Ember loved the fact that she finally met someone who would take her out and who could drive and come see her instead of her having to pick him up. And he paid for everything. The first night was the beginning of him taking her to nice places. They started going all over New York and New Jersey to nice places. Ember made sure to make him think that she was used to being treated nicely and being wined and dined. She acted as if it was expected instead of telling him she never had anyone take her out without her having to pay for them despite having been in what she thought were relationships. Ember enjoyed going out with Oscar so much that every time he called, no matter what, she would drop everything and make herself available.

On one of their dates, they went out to a restaurant. As they were eating, she asked him where he worked. He responded by saying, "In New York." Ember rephrased the question and said, "What do you do for work?" He pulled her close and whispered, "I am a cop." She asked him, "Why is it a secret? Are you undercover?" Oscar said, "No, I just didn't want you to say it loud." Ember loved the fact he had a good job and everything going for him. It was a big difference from all the criminals she went out with before. Ember wondered why it had to be a secret. Don't most cops like to brag about their job? When the waiter came, Oscar said, "I will have a virgin Pina Colada, virgin like me." She was beginning to believe that was true because he hadn't made a move on her yet. Then, he told her he was getting a BMW and "When girls try to holla, I am going to say I have a man." Ember figured he meant he had a woman so she didn't correct him or ask him what he meant.

They dated for six months before she began wondering why he never tried to have sex with her or even kiss her. She was not the type to ever make the first move so she figured she would just wait. Anyway, she was so happy that he was being respectful. While they were dating, she planned a trip to Mexico with her mom and sister. When she told Oscar she was going, he asked, "Are the guys there hot?" Ember figured he was asking to see what the competition was for him. She told him there was nothing for him to worry about. He said he just wanted to know because his "Best best guy friend told him guys over there were cute." She thought he was joking so she laughed about it even though it didn't make sense. He then asked her to take pictures of herself for him while she was on vacation.

She took sexy pictures, some in her bikini, and put them in a photo album that she bought in Mexico. When she got back home, she gave the album to him. A few days later, he called her and said the guys at the police station where he was a cop thought she was hot. She asked him when they saw her and he said, "I have your pictures up in my locker at work." Ember was so happy, figuring he was taking her seriously.

One night, while they were out, he said, "I would kiss you, but I don't want to mess up your lipstick." Ember thought to herself, "It's not lipstick- it's lip gloss, and even if it were lipstick, mess it up!" But she played it cool.

For another date, she met him at a restaurant uptown. Ember wore a dress, and he held her hand as they walked in after he gave her roses that he had bought for her. She thought he was perfect. She told all her friends, her mom, and her sister about him. They couldn't wait to meet him.

One day, Ember and Oscar were food shopping near his house, and they stopped for lunch. He told her he felt "meat was the devil" so he ordered a salad since he was a vegetarian. Ember was hungry so she ordered a roast beef sandwich, hoping not to offend him. When their food came, before she could blink, half of her sandwich was gone. He had eaten it. Ember told him she thought he had said, "Meat was the devil." He replied, "It's ok to eat it sometimes." Ember began thinking that he was a little strange for a few reasons. The meat situation was weird, the fact that he hadn't tried to get with her, and the way he wore platform shoes with a little heel was strange. She figured the shoes were because she was taller than him.

She met Oscar's mom before he met hers. After lunch, they visited his mom who worked at a furniture store. Ember couldn't believe he introduced her to his mom. Things must be getting more serious, she thought. She was pretty sure he was going to ask her to be his girl soon. His mom was nice and seemed to like Ember. He told her if she ever needed furniture, he could get her a discount.

That night, they went to his apartment. He lived with his sister. Ember met her as she was leaving to go see her boyfriend. She was really getting to know the family. After his sister left, they watched a movie. Then, he held her hand and walked her to his room where they had sex for the first time. It didn't last long, and his dick was small and crooked, but Ember didn't care. She liked him and wanted him to like her too.

After they had sex, he showed her pictures from his last trip to Puerto Rico and told her he wanted to take her there one day. Then, he reached into his drawer and gave her earrings that he told her he picked out just for her. Just as Ember thought she was special, until she looked over and saw a plastic bag full of similar earrings. She guessed maybe they were for his family, so she didn't ask and didn't jump to any conclusions.

Every time after that, Ember would get all dressed up, wear lingerie under her clothes, go over to his apartment, and have sex. She would never cum but, at the time, she thought it was good because he always came fast and would be embarrassed, which she thought meant he was sprung. She would sleep over a lot and drive an hour to work in the morning.

Ember paid for the bill when they went out once and that was the worst thing she could have ever done. After that time, he began expecting her to pay. Oscar had previously told her that he made over $100,000 a year and she wondered why he couldn't continue to pay when they went out. Ember realized she was doing the same thing with him that she did with other guys- paying her way and showing him that she didn't need anyone to pay for her or take her out. She figured out that she was doing this because she felt guilty when someone paid for her because of the way her dad treated her. Her dad made her feel guilty that he had to pay child support for her and her sister ever since she was five years old. She didn't want anyone else to be able to make her feel bad about taking her out or buying her things. But it was too late. Oscar was already used to her paying, and he expected it.

Her 25th birthday came around and she wanted to spend it with Oscar in a nice hotel in New Jersey. When he said he wasn't sure if he could make it, she told him she would pay. How pathetic was she? She was paying for someone to hang out with her on her birthday. She paid but told everyone he did so she didn't look or feel as bad about it.

Oscar came to pick her up at her house to go to the hotel. He went inside and met Ember's mom and her sister. Then, they were off to a lover's hotel. While there, they drank champagne, had sex, and spent time together. When they got back, her mom told her she was expecting to see a beautiful man show up, from the way Ember described him. She told her that she was too pretty for him, adding that she and her sister could not stop laughing when they saw him. He wasn't even friendly and seemed shy. She questioned whether he was really a cop. Ember was mad at her for this. Ember would soon see she was right but didn't want to admit it.

After a while, Oscar stopped calling Ember. She began calling him, wondering what was wrong. He said he had to work a lot more and didn't have much time to hang out. She believed him until she went out with her friend Alicia one day and saw his car parked outside the club. When they got inside, he was there talking to a girl who was taller than Ember. Alicia said the girl looked like a "man bitch." Oscar got nervous when he saw Ember and realized he had lied about working. He went up to her, kissed her on the cheek, told her she looked beautiful, and left. Before he left, Ember asked him for her pictures back. Even though they weren't naked pictures or anything, she wanted them back because they were her pictures. She had given them to him thinking he was going to be her boyfriend. He said he was going to give them back but never did. Why would he want her pictures if he didn't want to be with her? Ember got six numbers that night, but it didn't matter because the man she liked didn't like her. What did she do to make this happen?

After seeing him at the club that night, he called her from time to time but rarely asked her to go out. She began seeing him at almost every club or after-work party and he would avoid her. She realized his best friend, Tom, never really liked her and was always mean to her. Could that be why he was avoiding her?

Then, one day, Ember and Alicia went clubbing and saw him there with a different guy friend. His friend flirted with Ember, not knowing she used to talk to Oscar. Ember started flirting back on purpose. Alicia asked the guy why his friend (Oscar) ran away. His friend said he didn't know why. Alicia said, "Is he gay?" He said, "What gave it away? The fact that he is wearing a pink shirt and doesn't want to talk to pretty girls?" Ember took down his friend's number with the hopes of finding out more about Oscar. She called his friend, and they hung out. She kept asking him about Oscar. He told Ember he really thought Oscar was gay or at least bisexual and that his best friend was probably really his boyfriend. He also said Oscar was a security guard, not a police officer. Ember almost died. Could it be true? Now she realized that her meeting his family and him showing her pictures at work was probably all a front so no one would catch onto the fact he was gay. And, the fact that he wore platform shoes and asked her about other men was not because she was taller than him or because he was jealous. It was because he was gay.

She accepted it and stopped talking to him, but it bothered her. Ember remembered that his mom mentioned that his brother worked at a specific restaurant in New York. She looked his brother up online and saw what he looked like. Ember went to the restaurant where he worked and sat at his table by herself, pretending she was waiting for someone else. When she was about to leave, his brother asked her for her number. Her heart was beating fast as she gave it to him. They started talking about a gym close by and he said, "A lot of gay people work out there." Ember said, "I went out with a gay guy once without knowing he was gay." He replied, "He must have been bisexual." Ember knew stalking his brother was crazy, but she had to know. It was just a coincidence that his brother asked her for her number. Maybe he had the same taste as his older brother? Or maybe he knew she dated his brother because he had seen her pictures too?

A few months after meeting his brother, Oscar called Ember and asked her if she wanted to go to his house. She asked why he hadn't called in so long, and he said it was because he was mad that she flirted with his friend in front of his face. Ember knew that wasn't the reason because he stopped calling her way before that. Either way, she dropped everything once again and went over. When she got there, they hung out, went shopping, and then he said he had to go to his mom's house to give his brother something. Ember almost shit her pants. They drove to his mom's house and his brother came outside. She put her sunglasses on and sunk down into her seat. She was sure he would recognize her but hoped he would think it was a coincidence. He didn't say anything. Ember went home later that day and never heard from Oscar again.

About six months later, Oscar called her and told her not to call him anymore because he had a girlfriend. Ember told him she hadn't been calling him at all, and he said he felt he had to tell her just in case she thought of calling him. Ember was upset and still wondering. The whole situation got out of hand. She had no idea whether he was gay or whether she had ruined it trying to find out. One thing she did know was that it was completely over. Ember realized that if she had to wonder, he must not have ever liked her. If she had all those questions, she should not have taken him seriously because he obviously wasn't taking her seriously.

Years later, when Oscar was the last thing on Ember's mind, and she was clubbing with her friends, Oscar was at the same club with his same best friend. He tugged at her dress and said, "Hey, it's Oscar." Ember kept dancing with her friends as if he wasn't there.

Another time, after that, she saw him at a club with a girl. She realized that the girl was wearing the same style earrings he had given Ember from Puerto Rico when they were dating. She was grinding on him, and he looked happy until he saw Ember and Alicia. When he noticed them, he disappeared within a blink of an eye. Alicia said he had to be embarrassed because Ember got prettier throughout the years, and he was still wearing his platform shoes with a half-buttoned, button-down shirt. Ember realized, just like with every other guy she had ever dated, she gave him too much credit before really getting to know him. She learned that he was the same type of dude, just one who was dating all different genders.

CHAPTER SEVEN

Terrible Tyler

After weeks of being on the couch upset over the fact that Oscar didn't want her, Ember decided to go out and have fun. She called her friend Shanna, and she said she knew a good place in New York where they could go to dance and have a great time. Ember put on the shortest, tightest pair of shorts she owned, the highest heels she could find, and the sexiest shirt in her closet. She was ready to go out.

They got to the club and there weren't many guys there. While they were there, her friend kept saying it was a great club. Ember decided to ask her what she felt makes a club great. She said the music and the atmosphere. Ember thought to herself, "What does she know? She has a boyfriend. Who the hell cares about the music and the damn atmosphere? I need some eye candy right about now! Then, it would be a good club." Shanna called her boyfriend after a while and said she had to go home because he was there waiting for her. Ember was so glad she got that call because that meant they could leave. As they left the club, Ember quickly learned that all the cute guys were outside. There was a sexy, light-skinned baldy with green eyes who was nicely dressed outside waiting on line to get in. He yelled something out to Ember, and she looked back but kept walking because she didn't want to look desperate. Shanna stopped walking and said, "What are you, crazy? That is the cutest guy I have ever seen, and he wants to talk to you. Go over there now unless you want to lose the opportunity of a lifetime." As Ember looked back at him again, he was still looking at her. So, they walked over to him and his friends. He asked Ember for her name and number. His name was Tyler. He said he was from Union City. Ember had previously said she would never date anyone from Union City again, as she tended to meet all losers from there. But, she would make an exception just this one time. They exchanged numbers and she walked away. As they walked away, a guy in a car called Ember over. Shanna said, "You better not dare go over there or he will think you are desperate walking over to his car." So, she didn't. He jumped out of the car and gave Ember his number. Shanna, to her surprise, started promoting her. As he said, "You are so pretty," she said, "And she has a master's degree and a good job." Even though it was true, Ember couldn't understand why she would tell him all of that. She said that she wanted him to know Ember was more than just a "clubber." She was giving Ember advice on how to kick it to guys when she had a boyfriend and did the total opposite. Either way, Ember got two numbers that night and was happy.

The next day, Tyler called her and asked if she wanted to go on a date with him the following weekend. Ember quickly said yes and was very excited. She was so excited that she spent the rest of the week getting an outfit together. On the following Friday, he called and told her where they were going. Ember had never heard of the place. She was so happy to be going out on a date. She thought she would never find anyone other than Oscar to take her out on a date. Ember thought, "Now, only if he drove and had a car like Oscar, I would be ecstatic." The two planned to meet at 9 pm and, at exactly 8:59 pm, he called and said he was outside. Ember walked outside and was shocked to learn there was an Escalade in the driveway. She got in the car and was more than ecstatic. Not only did he drive, he drove an Escalade. He looked scrumptious and smelled amazing.

They got to the place and Ember had one drink while he had a few. He asked her why she didn't have a boyfriend, and she began talking about Oscar. Ember knew it wasn't a good idea to talk about another guy on their first date, but she couldn't help it. She was still not over it and was still questioning why things were the way they were with Oscar. After some time, his friends showed up with their girlfriends. He introduced Ember and everyone seemed nice. One of his friend's girlfriends told her that Tyler was nice and single too. They danced a little bit, but he seemed bothered by the fact that she wore high heels and was slightly taller than him because of it.

During the night, he went to the bathroom and Ember was approached by a guy who asked her, "Do you want to dance now that your boyfriend is in the bathroom?" She declined and, as he was talking to her, Tyler walked out of the bathroom. The guy walked away from Ember and Tyler quickly asked her why he was talking to her. Before she could answer, Tyler went over to his friends. Then, the guy came over to him, they said something to each other, and Tyler gave him a pound. Tyler walked back over to Ember and said, "I was going to fuck him up for disrespecting me, but he saved himself by telling me that he wasn't trying to be disrespectful, but he wanted to compliment me for having the prettiest girl in the club." Ember was amazed and so happy that happened. It was great that someone gave her such a wonderful compliment. Now, if he hadn't already noticed, Tyler knew she was beautiful and would want her around. At the end of the night, their bill came, and it was $120. She only had one drink and offered to give him $20. He took the money and said she was the first girl to ever offer to pay for herself and he liked that. He drove her home after what she thought was the perfect night.

The next day, she received a call from him saying that she had forgotten her heels in his car when she put her flip-flops on at the end of the night. He said he had them hanging from his rearview mirror and they laughed. Then, he said he told everyone he was happy because he met a "big bitch." Her laughter quickly faded, and she asked what he had meant by that. He said, "Well, you are tall, and I told everyone you are my big bitch." When they hung up, she told her mom and she said, "Well, you are tall with your heels, and it seems that he has a silly sense of humor." She said to ignore it because he probably meant it in a joking way. Besides, maybe Ember had to "stop being so sensitive", as her mom would always say. So, Ember did try to forget about it.

When he didn't call her for a week, Ember wondered why. She thought their first date was great. The fact that another guy liked her, and he got upset, seemed like a good thing to her. Ember was on her way to a salsa class with her friend Alicia three weeks later when he called. He said he was with his friends at a lounge and asked her if she wanted to meet him. Ember asked Alicia if she wanted to go after the class and she said she would. After coming back from the city, they went to where he was. He bought her a drink and her friend began talking to his friend. They danced a little and the place was closing. His friend said he would drive Alicia home, but Ember said she would do it. As they got into Ember's car, Alicia said she wanted to go with his friend. Ember told her she offered to drive her because she wasn't sure if Alicia liked him. Alicia said she didn't but he drove a Mercedes so she would go. Ember drove home, and he took Alicia home. Tyler wanted her to hang out with him, but she had to go home to get some rest for work the next day.

A few days went by, and Alicia called Ember while she was out with Tyler. She sounded very upset. She said that she asked Tyler's friend to pick her up from work. When he picked her up, he thought they were going to hang out and she said she just needed a ride home, so he cursed her out and left her in the middle of New York. She also said that he mentioned Tyler wanted to go to a hotel with Ember. She also said that they had a conversation about the fact that she said she liked nice handbags, and he responded by saying he liked nice cars and sex. Alicia ended the conversation by saying that Tyler's friend had balls. She said Tyler could get away with something like that because he was cute, but his friend was ugly and had no right to be an asshole. Tyler heard the conversation with Alicia and called his friend who was furious because Alicia made him go from New Jersey to New York to pick her up. Ember hung up with Alicia and Tyler hung up with his friend. Tyler asked her if she wanted to go to a hotel and drink, just as Alicia said he would. Not listening to Alicia's warning, she said she would (even though she really didn't drink). Ember was unsure of what the outcome would be since Alicia just had a bad experience with his friend.

They got to the hotel. It wasn't a fancy hotel. It was actually a motel. But Ember didn't care because it was an opportunity for them to talk and get to know each other. At the end of all their talking, they ended up having sex. It took two pumps, and he was done. Then, they got up, didn't say anything to each other, and he drove her home. On the way home, he blasted a song that kept repeating "ella no quiero novio (She doesn't want a boyfriend)." and Ember felt like crying. She basically fucked him on the second date. She did not know whether she should call him, wait for him to call her, or lie down and die. This was all new to her. She had sex with him so soon and he wasn't her boyfriend. Would she ever see him again? Would he think she was a whore? Would he be her boyfriend in the future? She couldn't stand being in suspense, so she called him the next day. After a brief conversation, he said he would call her soon. She felt that at least she called so she wouldn't look completely bad and so he wouldn't think she was a whore or a one-night stand.

After a month of being tortured by waiting for his call, Ember gave up. She was a mess, but he didn't know it. It was the first time she had sex with someone who didn't want something more from her. She thought Oscar was bad but at least he took her out on dates after they had sex, and he had the courtesy to call her the next day.

She had set the stage and made him think she was going to pay for everything after their first date. She thought she was doing a good thing by giving him $20 for her drink. In reality, it was the worst thing she could have ever done. Now, he would invite her to dinner and expect her to pay. After about two months, Tyler called her and asked if she wanted to take him out to eat at an Italian restaurant that he had always wanted to go to. Ember said she would. On the day they were supposed to go, she waited for his call. They were supposed to meet at 8 pm. At 10 pm, he called and said he broke his hip playing football and was in the hospital. He said that, as he was in the air trying to catch the ball, he thought, "Oh, no- my date. She is going to be so mad" before he hit the ground and hurt himself. Ember told him she didn't believe him. He said he would have to be crazy to make something up like that. She said it was ok and told him to call her when he was better.

Tyler called her again after recovering from his "injury" and asked her to hang out. Ember got all excited, got an outfit ready, bought lingerie, and got her hair and nails done. What Alicia had once told her was right: "Whether it is after a day, a week, a month, or a year, men always call back."

Ember figured this time she would put it on him and make an impression. They went to a hotel again and she got ready in the bathroom for about half an hour- body shimmer, perfume, lingerie, everything. After a week of preparing to have sex with him, he came with two pumps again and was ready to leave. When he first met up with her that night, he had a limp because of his hip. When he left, the limp went away, probably because he forgot his hip was supposed to be broken and healing. Ember was pissed but confused. She thought she could win him over and make him like her more with sex like she did with Oscar for a while, but he obviously didn't like her. He just wanted to use her. It was too late- Ember liked him. She made herself believe he liked her by holding onto the fact that he came with two pumps- he had to think she was sexy, right? After that night, she decided she would not have sex with him again unless he took her out.

Ember invited Tyler and his friend over one night when her mom was on vacation. His friend came over and tried to get with her sister, but she didn't like him. After staying for a little bit, Tyler and his friend decided to leave and said they were going to come back. Ember called Tyler to see when they were coming back, and he said he decided to go home instead. His friend then called her and asked her if she wanted to have a threesome with him and Tyler. As pissed as she was, she said yes just to see if Tyler would come back. And he did. They pulled up in front of her house and she went outside. His friend told her to get in the car. Ember looked at Tyler and said, "You're a pig." He told his friend to drive off, adding, "She's a bitch. Let's just leave." Ember went inside and cried. She thought, "How could he ever think I was like that? I liked him. I would never have sex with him and his friend. He must have no respect for me."

About a half a year went by and they didn't speak. He called her one night when she was out with her friend and her sister and said he wanted to meet up with her to talk. Ember's sister and friend told her she should go, as she looked very pretty. Ember decided to go. When he got out of his car to approach her, Ember's sister looked at him and said, "I hate you." He laughed and she did too. Then, Ember got into his car, and he said he was sorry and the only reason he went back to her house that night with his friend was because he wanted to see if she really was serious. Ember was still pissed but at least he apologized. Then, he asked her if she wanted to go to a hotel. She told him she had her period, and he said, "I will go through the red light." Ember responded and said, "So, you will eat the red light?" and he laughed. The fact was that he always asked her to give him head and then wouldn't kiss her after. He never once performed oral sex on her and it pissed her off. He should have tried to because it may have made up for his two pumps and small penis. Either way, he drove her home, and they said good-bye until next time.

The next time they went to a hotel, it was to celebrate his birthday. Even though she didn't even get a phone call on her birthday from him after reminding him it was her birthday for about a month, Ember decided to buy him a bottle of his favorite liquor and wrote him a poem. They got to the hotel, and she gave him the bottle and the card with the poem in it. The poem went like this:

> It all started at Gypsey Tea when you decided to holla at me.
>
> My friend was mad because I walked away
>
> Then, she hid behind me when you walked over because she didn't know what to say
>
> A big bitch is what you told your friends you met
>
> I have to admit, when you told me that, I was kind of upset
>
> We went out that weekend

You, me, and your friends

That dude tried to holla at me when you were out of sight

Little did he know, you were ready to fight

You should've listened to him when he said I was the prettiest girl that night

You drank like 20 rum and cokes

Then, we went to IHOP for Viva la French Toast

You waited awhile to call me

I had taken your number out of my phone and asked myself, "Who could this be?"

That was the day me and my friends met you and your friend

I don't think I have to say much more- I think we both thought that was the end

We decided to chill anyway

And we had sex that day

You never held back

My ass you said you wanted to smack

I hoped you would call again and not make the situation into a mess

But I decided I wasn't going to stress

I called you the next day

And I hoped with my heart you weren't going to play

I was scared because I didn't want to be a booty call

And for you I thought I was beginning to fall

You turned out to be a real cool dude-

Someone I could call when I am in the mood

After that, we had sex a few more times

I told you how much I wished you were mine

You said you liked to chill but had other friends

I continued to talk to you because I didn't want it to end

I know you thought you had it made when we had sex in back of your Escalade

You must have liked me a lot

Because, unlike other girls, we had sex in your parking spot

But it almost came to an end when you couldn't control your friend

You thought I was wild but you were wrong

That night, to each other, we all said good-bye, so long

I wished you were a little more into me

But I accepted that was the way it had to be

A few months later, I guess we were thinking about each other when you called

We met up, my sister told you she hates you, and you were appalled

I was wearing a sexy dress

We wondered what would happen next

We cleared things up and had make up sex

We hung out last year for your birthday

We went out and then I showed you my lingerie

You need to know that one of the reasons I decide to chill with you

Is because inside and out, you are beautiful

Hopefully, there are more good times to come

With you, I always have fun

He read the poem, and they drank and had sex. When they were ready to leave, he took the bottle with him and left the card with the poem behind. Ember was so annoyed. She had put a lot of hard work into it and, even if he didn't like it, he should have taken it. Her mom was right- he liked alcohol more than anything else. Ember slammed the door of his Escalade when he dropped her off at home and left without saying good- bye.

The next time he called, he asked her if she was mad at him, and she told him she was because he left the poem behind. He said that when he noticed he didn't take it, he tried to go back, and it wasn't there. He asked her to meet him at a club that night. He said he would be there with his friend and said Ember should bring her friends. Ember really didn't have anyone to bring so she went through her whole phone book and dug up everyone she knew. She usually went out with Alicia, but she couldn't bring her around him anymore. Ember finally convinced one of her friends to go out with her. They got there and he did his thing and talked to other girls, so Ember did her thing too. At the end of the night, he called her, and they ended up having sex. Yup, you guessed it- two pumps again and they were done. From then on, they continued meeting at clubs and having sex at the end of the night. He became a booty call- a bad one at that. But Ember kept him around because he was cute, and it was something to do. She also liked him and hoped something more would come out of it. As time went by, he would tell her that he wanted her to be his girlfriend, but he never actually did anything to make it happen. Ember had false hope and thought that if she was the best girl he ever had, he would want something more. She kept her feelings inside and continued to have sex with him and act as if she didn't like him. She figured no one wants a girl who is too clingy, right?

Just to paint a clear picture of what an idiot Tyler was, not only did he lose out in life by not making her his girlfriend, but he couldn't even remember the stupid lies he used to make up for no reason at all. He would go over to her apartment, have sex with her, and leave right away. One night, after having sex, he said he had to leave before rush hour traffic, either thinking Ember was stupid or forgetting it was 4 am on a Saturday in New Jersey. She knew he was just saying that because he needed an excuse for leaving right away so he didn't look like the asshole he was. Shortly after that, the next time they chilled, she told him about something Oscar once said that made no sense and he said he was stupid for saying that. She responded by saying, "Yeah. It was almost as stupid as someone saying they had to leave before hitting traffic at 4 am on a Saturday." He must have completely forgotten that he even said that or maybe he was drunk when he said it. Whatever the reason, he responded and said, "That is so stupid. What idiot said that?" He was stupid enough to lie and not smart enough to remember the lies. That wasn't the only lie he told her.

Every time Ember would bring it up, he would tell her he didn't have children. One of the nights they went clubbing, she told him that her friend who met him for the first time told her that he looked like he partied and had ten kids. He quickly reminded her that he didn't have any kids. When Ember moved, she asked him if he knew anyone who could help her, hoping that he would volunteer. She got the next best thing- he said his cousin would help her if she would pay him. When his cousin helped her, he asked her if she wanted to see a picture of Tyler's daughter. Ember replied, "Tyler has a daughter?" He nervously said, "Oh, no. I meant my daughter." Ember never got to see the picture. His cousin also said he didn't understand how Tyler and Ember talked, because she was not his type at all. He went on to say Ember was too tall and wore heels and Tyler liked short girls because he was insecure about his height. When she talked to Tyler the next day, Ember said, "Oh, I saw a picture of your daughter. She is so big." Not realizing he previously assured her he did not have any kids, he said, "Yes, she is 16 already." Ember couldn't believe it. She said, "You never told me you had a daughter." He quickly said, "I don't." It was too late. He was caught in another lie. He was also looking unattractive. If a man denies his kids, why would he ever admit he has a girlfriend?

One thing was for sure- he would be her first and last booty call. His cousin summed it up- Tyler will never settle down, he drinks a lot, he doesn't want a relationship with anyone, and he is self-conscious about his height. After seven years, Ember realized it wasn't her. It was him. Her issue was being too available for him and not realizing he wasn't worth all her efforts.

One night, her intuition was put to the test when he invited her to a birthday party. When she got there, he was with another girl. Ember always thought he would have a beautiful girlfriend if he ever did decide to have a girlfriend because he was so handsome and sexy. This girl was a plain Jane. She wasn't pretty at all, and he was all over her. Ember felt like her world came shattering down. She brought her friends with her to celebrate his birthday, and he made her look like an idiot. Another guy, Carlos, came up to Ember and she quickly got over the fact that Tyler was with another girl. She realized this guy was a friend of Tyler's and she had seen him in pictures and thought he was cute. As Ember talked to him, he kicked it to her, and they exchanged numbers. She figured it wasn't a big deal, and she was starting to understand she had to live her own life.

As Ember was getting ready to go, Tyler went up to her and Carlos and tried to introduce them. When he realized they had already met without his help, he was pissed. He uttered something, placed his hand under her dress, and said, "Keep it tight." Ember was so upset. He was with another girl and made it look like she was the bad one. Carlos called her that night and told her he would bring breakfast to her house, but she declined. As much as she wanted to call Carlos, she didn't after that night because she figured there were other guys in the world other than Tyler's friends and it just wasn't worth it.

When Ember got outside of the club that night, Tyler was there with a different girl next to him. He was bleeding from his forehead and had blood on his shirt. When she asked if he was okay, the girl screamed out, "He is fine." Ember thought to herself, "I know he is. That is why I got with him." He looked nervous and told her to just leave. When she called him later, he said that girl was his ex-girlfriend's cousin, and she hit him over the head with a bottle when she saw him talking to other girls. He said he didn't know why she would do that, as they haven't been together in over three years. It sounded weird but Ember just believed it. Denial is a bitch.

When Tyler told her he was going to the military, Ember decided to make him a poster with pictures of him, her, and his friends and have all his friends sign it before he left. They went clubbing and she had the poster outside. She asked all his friends to go outside to sign it. He started getting mad, asking why she was talking to all his boys. Ember just ignored it, knowing he would be happy when he found out why. His friend's girlfriend hated Ember for some reason (probably because she was much prettier than her). When she came outside, she told his friend, "You are not signing that for that bitch." Ember thought, "What a hater." No one wanted her man- he was a pig anyway. He was the same friend who tried to have a threesome with her. But she kept that to herself, smiled, looked at her, and politely said, "Hey, would you like to sign?" while handing her the marker. She looked furious and said, "No, I don't want to sign that shit." She probably wanted to fight but knew Ember would win. Little did she know Ember wouldn't fight her because it wasn't worth her time.

When she gave Tyler the poster at the end of the night, he looked like he wanted to cry. He said it was the nicest thing that anyone ever did for him. But it still didn't get her girlfriend status.

When Tyler left for boot camp, he wrote to Ember and said he needed sneakers. So, she bought him sneakers and sent them to him. When he came back, he invited her to a party that he was having. Ember knew she had to wake up early the next day for work, but she said she would go. She went with her sister. Ember put on a gold dress that made her ass look huge and that was low cut, showing her breasts. She looked like a superstar. She felt so beautiful. Every guy in there wanted her and approached her. They hung out with Tyler and his friends. Towards the end of the night, Tyler asked her if she was going to let him come over. She told him she was just going to go home because she was tired and had to wake up early. He got so pissed, probably because he wasn't used to her saying no to him. He told his friend that he wanted to leave. He didn't even walk her and her sister to their car. As he walked in front of them, he put his arm out and said, "Fuck this bitch." His friend said, "He doesn't mean that." Ember knew why he was acting like that, and he was drunk too. So, she laughed and said, "Your tattoo of the flag with a star on your elbow is so wack anyway." Ember and her sister started cracking up and went home so she could get some rest.

The next time Ember went clubbing with Tyler, the tables turned. She wore a classy yet sexy hot pink, off-the-shoulder dress with pink high heels. Her hair was highlighted blonde, and her skin was sun-kissed. She was ready to go out and have fun without stressing over what Tyler was doing. When she walked into the club with her outfit and attitude, she was a showstopper. A lot of guys tried to dance with her. She felt pretty and confident. Tyler was there but she said hello and did not pay too much attention to him. Ember was giving him a taste of his own medicine. After about an hour of being there and meeting everyone she wanted to meet, Tyler came up to her and they danced. He told her how pretty she looked. While they were dancing, a guy she met at the beginning of the night tapped her on the shoulder and told her she had promised him a dance. Tyler didn't like that at all. He tugged her arm and said, "She's with me." The guy pulled her other arm and said he didn't care. As they were having a tug of war with both of her arms and she was laughing and flattered, the club promoter snapped a picture. Little did she know that picture would signify the beginning of how she gained control of the situation.

Ever since that day, Ember realized that she had the power to take control of the situation. The moment she decided to just do her, have fun, and not allow anyone to have control over her, she felt like a ton of bricks was lifted off her shoulders. For the first time, she didn't stress over whether he liked her or not. Obviously, he did like her. But just not enough to make her his girl. So, she had to move on. Ember realized if she had to wonder if he liked her and ask questions about it, he couldn't like her too much. She began to look at him in a different light. She began to enjoy her single life and the fact that she could have any guy she wanted, which is something she never believed before. Ember had such a different image of him, and she put him on a pedestal that he should have never been put on. From that day on, she didn't make herself available to him all the time. If she had something to do, she would do it and not drop anything for him. Every time he would ask her why she wore heels since she was already a "big bitch," she would stand even taller and be proud of who she was. She thought he should stop worrying about her being tall and start worrying about him being so short and coming in two pumps. Now, those were serious problems.

When she told everyone about his two pumps and that she didn't ever get anything out of having sex with him, they would ask her why she continued to stay and have sex with him. Ember never really had a good answer to that. She was still looking for something more. Ember was staying around hoping one day he would like her and take it to the next level. It was kind of like the same way she was with her dad. She wished he would love her for her, but he only liked her for what she could do for him. When she was giving her dad money, he was comfortable and good. When she didn't, he was evil and chased her until he got what he wanted. Similarly, with Tyler, when Ember gave him what he wanted, he was nice and became comfortable. When she made him work for it, he would chase her to get what he wanted.

After getting advice from her sister's boyfriend at the time who said it would be a good idea to initiate sex with Tyler one time, Ember decided to take control for once instead of waiting for him to call her. She called him and they met up. They decided to have sex in his car. They climbed into the back seat of his Escalade. She had a dress on. She jumped on his dick at 2:21 am and he was finished at 2:21 am. Just when she thought two pumps was bad, she learned it had gotten worse. So, Ember jumped into the front seat as soon as he was done and told him she was ready to go. He was still trying to catch his breath in the back seat and could barely believe what happened. Instead of being embarrassed, as she thought he would, she realized that he didn't care about pleasing her. Any other guy would be mortified and would try to redeem himself. But not Tyler.

Ember was tired of him calling the shots and the sex was horrible. She began to get bored with the sex and would hang out with him to fulfill her need of talking and hanging out but would end the night before having sex. The first time she did this, he was furious. It must have been that he thought he had it like that. When he realized he didn't, he couldn't handle it.

One night, he called Ember and asked her if she wanted to hang out. Initially, she said she would. As the night went on and she thought about it, Ember decided that two pumps was not enough to make her want to hang out and be tired the next day. She texted him and told him she had changed her mind and didn't want to hang out. This was the first time she did this. He responded and said, "How about I come over for a quickie?" Ember said, "What would make that different from any other time?" The next thing she knew, he was blowing up her phone. Soon enough, he was at her door. Ember didn't answer and could care less what the outcome would be. Her sleep was more important than a meaningless two pump booty call.

Time went by and Tyler would call her and try to make plans. Sometimes, she would go and sometimes she wouldn't, depending on how she felt and whether she had other plans or not. This whole "relationship" went on for about seven years on and off. Ember was with other guys in between and in relationships but she knew she could always hang out with Tyler if she wanted to. They began hanging out less because she began losing interest. Yeah, he was cute. But cute wasn't everything. Ember needed something more. Something he couldn't give her. So, she moved on.

If she had to describe her relationship with Tyler, it would go something like this: they would hang out, he would drink, they would talk, he would tell her how much he wanted her to be something more, he would make future plans to do fun things that they never ended up doing, they would have sex, and then he would leave. Ember would patiently wait for the next time to see him, even though it was only two pumps. She learned that if you must guess if someone likes you, he doesn't. She should have been able to be herself. She didn't have to go out of her way to please him. She wished she would've learned this earlier. It took seven years to learn this hard lesson, but it was something she would never go through again in her life now that she knew. So, it was worth it.

They hung out after Ember decided to really move on. She brought her friend to a bar to watch a football game with him, as he invited her out. They hadn't seen each other in so long. He was so happy to see her.

That night, her friend got his cousin's number. No one thought anything about it. Ember left knowing she didn't feel the same way about Tyler. She realized she was over him. He pointed out the fact that a woman behind her was staring at her ass. He made a big deal of it and said it was so nice that everyone had to stare at it. In front of all his friends, he also made sure to mention that Ember used to jump for everything in the past and now, he calls her and reaches her voicemail almost every time. Ember knew it was because she was finally over him.

A few days after going out and watching the football game, her friend went on a date with Tyler's cousin and couldn't wait to tell her about it. They continued dating and, after a while, she got invited to family functions. One day, she called Ember and said that Tyler called his cousin, and he let her friend answer. When she answered, he asked who she was and she said, "It's Lisa." He said that Lisa and his cousin were invited to a New Year's Eve party. She asked where it would be, and he said it would be at his girlfriend's house. When Lisa told Ember this, she didn't know what to think. Ember was kind of relieved because maybe he acted the way he did toward her in the past because he had a girlfriend, not because he didn't like her. She was also surprised that she didn't find out about her sooner, as they had been dealing with each other for seven years. When Tyler found out it was Ember's friend he had invited to the party, she was quickly uninvited. He must not have put together that the Lisa who answered his cousin's phone was Ember's friend. He was mad that he was stupid enough to invite her friend to his girlfriend's party-a girlfriend she never knew he had.

Lisa was soon invited to a get-together at Tyler's dad's house. Without Ember knowing, she asked if Ember could go and was told she couldn't. When Ember found out, she was mad that Lisa asked if she could attend the party. She didn't want it to look as though she was asking to go because she wasn't. Ember told her friend to never mention her again.

Lisa called Ember one day and said that she talked to Tyler's aunt, who was her boyfriend's mom, and she was saying that Lisa may have problems with her son's baby mom in the future because she is crazy. Lisa mentioned that she had met her son's baby mom in the past. His mom asked Lisa when they met, and she said they met a while ago at IHOP with Tyler and her friend (who was Ember). His mom then asked who Lisa's friend was and she mentioned Ember's name. His mom then said, "I know about her. The one with the blonde hair with the job in law enforcement? Tyler was in love with that girl." Lisa responded by saying, "Really?" His aunt said, "Yes. He used to talk about her all the time but he has had a girlfriend for seven years who the family hates and who is obsessed with him and provides for him so that is why it never became serious between him and your friend."

Tyler's cousin cleared everything up. Tyler never broke his leg, but his cousin found it funny when Ember told him how Tyler told her he was worried about their date when he was mid-air on the football field. Tyler may have liked Ember, but he was with his girlfriend for seven years. It turns out his girlfriend ended up being the same girl who hit him over the head with the bottle in the club. His cousin added that his girlfriend does everything for him, including paying his bills. Their family had labeled his girlfriend as "crazy." However, Ember knew he was the crazy one. The only thing that made her crazy was the fact that she stayed with him knowing what he was about. At the end of it all, Ember had to give Tyler credit for keeping the lies up for such a long time and for not letting his girlfriend find out about Ember and vice versa for seven years. Ember knew all of Tyler's friends. She wondered why none of them told her about his girlfriend or his girlfriend about her. In the end, who cares? It was two pumps while it lasted and he was her problem, not Ember's. He still hit Ember up, but she refused to answer. If a guy has a girlfriend and the sidepiece doesn't know about it, it is one thing. Now that Ember knew the deal, she would never pick up for him again.

All the questions she had in the past were finally answered. Part of her wanted to call him and the other part wanted to leave it alone. If he really liked her that much, he would've done something about it. She came to realize that he liked her the same way she liked him. They were both just too stubborn to admit it and now it was too late. She thought, even if he wasn't in a relationship, she was so over him already that it wouldn't even matter. It was a wonderful feeling knowing that he liked her, though, and that it wasn't because of anything she did that he didn't make her his girl.

About two years after they stopped talking, Ember happened to see him at a local supermarket. It was Thanksgiving Day, and she had stopped in for a ham steak to buy her dad because she was going to visit him, and she knew he didn't eat turkey. She was in a rush and looked like crap. Her hair was in a ponytail, she had a baggy shirt on, and she barely had any makeup on. She just stopped in before she got all dressed up for dinner. As she walked through the aisle, she saw Tyler. Ember tried to avoid him seeing her, but he began walking after her and calling her name. He said, "I guess this is the only way I can see you since you don't answer any of my texts." Ember smiled and walked away. She called her friend when she left and was a little upset because he caught her off guard on a bad day. Her friend told her not to worry because one bad day wouldn't cancel out seven years of great days every time she saw him. She ended up being wrong.

He was a superficial loser who had to put others down to boost his ego every time he got dissed. A few weeks later, Lisa told Ember that Tyler said he saw her, and she had gained weight. Ember had gained a few pounds but not the way he made it sound. Also, she was wearing a baggy shirt that day and didn't have high heels on. Ember was so pissed. She knew it shouldn't have mattered, but it did. Ember decided to go to the gym where she knew he worked out, let him see he was wrong, and make him feel stupid about it. So, when she saw him at the gym and every guy was looking at her because of how in shape she was, he tried to talk to her. She loudly said in front of everyone, "I guess I was able to lose a few pounds. Too bad it isn't as easy to grow a dick." He looked at her and his face turned red. He didn't even know his cousin had told her friend that before she said anything. Ember walked away with a smile on her face. She had gotten the last laugh. It felt good.

CHAPTER EIGHT

Victorious Vincent

Ember used to have a crush on a guy named Vincent in grammar school. He never knew it, though, because he was one of the "cool" kids and she was a "nerd." While reminiscing one night, she brought up his name to her friend Sophie. Sophie said she was friends with one of his friends. At the time, Ember had just finished her first master's degree and was working in the law enforcement field. He would be surprised to learn she grew up to be a nerd in disguise, as she was smart but pretty, too. Sophie said she would set up a date for them to meet and hang out. She told Ember not to mention where she worked because she thought he may have a criminal record and was afraid it might scare him away.

Sophie set up the date. They met at a pool hall. He was still so handsome. As they talked, he asked her where she worked, and she lied and told him she was a secretary. He responded and said, "That's good, I guess. You gotta do something with your life." Although being a secretary is a good career, it wasn't Ember's career, and she felt upset that she couldn't be herself while being around Vincent.

Vincent's friend, Lucas, who she also went to grammar school with, came by later and they began talking. He started talking about a girl named Sylvia who they all went to school with as well. Sylvia and Ember were always in competition for first place in the spelling bee, as she was smart like Ember. The only difference between Ember and Sylvia in grammar school was that Sylvia had big boobs, and the guys liked her. Lucas went on to tell Ember that Sylvia was married with a child and had a successful career as a banker as well. When he asked Ember what she was doing, she had to tell him she was a secretary because she had already told Vincent that was what she did. What she really wanted to tell him was the truth- that she was working on her second master's degree and had a job in the law enforcement field while also going to nursing school as a backup plan. The only real difference between Ember and Sylvia was that she was married now with a child and Ember was still dating dumbass dudes. Oh, how Ember wanted to brag about her education and her wonderful job. Ember had learned her lesson: Don't ever hide your accomplishments to cater to someone else.

Vincent and Ember continued texting each other after that night. Every time he would text her, it would seem like he only wanted sex and wasn't interested in a relationship, so she didn't hang out with him for a while. Then, one day, with the advice of one of her friends, she decided she was going to have sex with him. When he texted her next asking her to hang out, she said okay. He said she should tell him when and he would plan where. Ember was away for work and was coming up for the weekend, so they planned to see each other. He rented a hotel room at the Days Inn. It was summertime and she wore shorts, a halter top, and high heels. When he saw her, he looked so happy, and she felt so pretty.

He attacked her in the elevator, kissing her and putting his hands all over her. They had sex as soon as they got into the room. They did it three times. His dick was big, and the sex was great. He ate her out and even talked Spanish while they were doing it. Ember thought she was in love, but she kept telling herself to play it cool, remembering that he didn't seem to want a girlfriend. After they were done, with her friend's advice, she began getting dressed. He was lying in bed with a perplexed look and asked her where she was going. Ember told him she had to catch the next flight back to training in South Carolina. He said he had the room for the whole night. She told him she had to leave, although every part of her wanted to stay. So, she left.

Ember was in suspense that night until the next morning when he texted her and said he had fun the night before and couldn't wait to see her again. They kept having sex, great sex. She didn't mind having him as a booty call because, unlike Tyler, he was a good booty call. Although, deep down inside, she wished it could be something more.

One night, he called her and said he got a new apartment in New Jersey near her and wasn't staying at his grandma's place in the Bronx anymore. He invited her and her friend Sophie over and said he would be there with some of his friends. He asked if she could buy a bottle of Hennessey and soda, and he would give her the money when she got there. Ember was hesitant because she didn't know if he would really give her the money back. She wondered why he couldn't buy it since he lived right near a liquor store. Ember decided to buy it and hoped for the best.

Ember told Sophie that the plan was for Ember to leave with her if he didn't give her the money for the bottle and she would stay if he did. They got there and drank a little. His friend left after a while. He put the bottle of Hennessy and the soda in the refrigerator, so Ember figured he wasn't planning on giving her the money. He went into his bedroom, and they heard a loud noise that sounded like a hair dryer. Sophie and Ember looked at each other and wondered what it was. He came back to the living room and said that he was sorry for the noise, but he was blowing up his bed. Sophie and Ember looked at each other again and began laughing. It was definitely time for them to leave. He asked Ember to stay but she told him she was leaving. He told her to call him if she changed her mind.

When the girls got downstairs, they realized he never mentioned paying Ember, so the bottle of Hennessey actually belonged to her. She called him and told him she was coming back upstairs. He sounded ecstatic. When she got back upstairs, he was standing there with his shirt off and his arm across the doorway thinking he was sexy. He said, "I knew you would come back." Ember walked right past him to the refrigerator and grabbed the bottle. As she got to the door, she walked back inside toward where he was standing near the kitchen and said, "I forgot one more thing." He winked at her, and she said, "Not you" as she took her soda out of the refrigerator. She left for the night. She just couldn't have one more person use her for money. She hated the feeling of being used. Why shouldn't he pay for his own bottle of liquor? She didn't even drink Hennessey.

Ember and Vincent didn't talk for months after that. One day, she got a text from him asking her to come over. As she was deciding whether she wanted to go, she got a second text from him saying, "You should buy us a little bottle of Ciroc." Ember texted back and said, "You should buy me a big bottle of Patron." He texted back, "I would but I don't have any cash." She sent the next text and said, "No cash=no Ciroc=no ass." He answered and said, "I don't like your math." Ember liked the fact that he was quick with it and the sex was good, but it wasn't worth the feeling that she was being taken advantage of; nothing was. So, she cut him off.

CHAPTER NINE

Not So Kind Keith

Ember took an LSAT class after she graduated college just to see if she wanted to go to law school. She also took it just to be in New York and to not miss out on any potential guys since the city is full of them. Ember picked her college because it was a well-known school but also because the ratio of guys to girls was 10-1 since it used to be a school primarily for police officers. Once she started attending, she learned it was more like 10 girls to every 1 not-so-hot guy. So, she had another strategy to meet men. She would get dressed up for school and take the bus there from New Jersey and then walk twenty blocks there and twenty blocks back in high heels to see who she would meet.

Ember used the same idea when she was on her way to her LSAT class. It was a summer afternoon, and she put on a cute new pair of high heels, a nice purple tank top, and some tight jeans and walked to class. She was hoping to see this cute guy who tried to talk to her the week before and who she thought worked for a security company near her school. As she walked by, Ember noticed he wasn't there. Instead, this guy passed by her, and she stared him in the eyes and smiled. He looked back at her as she passed by. About a block later, Ember noticed he was behind her. He tapped her on her shoulder and said he couldn't help but talk to her. Like all men she had met before, he said he usually didn't meet women that way, but he thought Ember was so pretty that he had to stop to talk to her. As they were walking, Ember stopped to get ice cream. He offered to buy it for her, but she paid for it herself. Ember told him that he was cute and that she would hook him up with her sister because he looked way too young for her. To her surprise, he was older than her. He just didn't look it because he was skinny and dressed as if he were younger. So, they exchanged numbers. She figured they could be good friends, if anything.

Keith called her a few days later and asked her to hang out. Ember met up with him in New York and they went to an Irish pub. They had fun. He told her he was single with no kids but didn't want to rush into anything. She told him it was the same situation with her.

As time went by, they continued meeting in the city and going places like out to eat, bowling, to the movies, and just anywhere that they could have fun and do new and exciting things. Ember had a lot of fun when she was with him. The only thing was that she lived with her mom, and he never asked her to go back to Brooklyn where he lived. She ended up getting her own apartment when they were together. He said he would give her money to move out into her first apartment. Ember kept going back and forth with the idea, worrying she may not be able to afford it. It would have been nice to have him help her, but she didn't want to feel as though she owed him anything. Ember ended up being forced to get her own apartment because of what happened with her sister and her getting arrested and not wanting to be in her mom's house anymore because of it. Keith came over the first night she was at her apartment, and it was a mess. She didn't even have a bed there, but they hung out.

As time passed, Ember realized Keith was starting to like her more. She liked him too. She knew he liked her because she would stare into his eyes every time they would talk, and he would unknowingly pull on his ear nervously every time. Ember knew she made him nervous, and he gave her butterflies. He would get compliments about her from random people everywhere they went. She met his friends, and they loved her. He worked in the fashion industry and would always compliment her style. He would also get her clothes from sample sales. He once got her this ugly shirt and wanted her to wear it when they went out. Ember was forced to wear it because she figured he might stop getting her things if he thought she didn't appreciate it. So, she wore it on one of their dates. He continued getting her clothes from his job. Keith was the first guy who ever thought of her in that way, who cared about her, and who was not looking for anything in return. Being with Keith was different. It was great and Ember was happy. She didn't want to ruin things by sleeping with him too quickly. She made him wait. He waited three months just to kiss her and six months before they had sex.

Ember couldn't possibly have sex with him the first few times he came to her apartment because he would think she was only holding out because she lived with her mom. So, he came over to her apartment and they didn't do anything. Until one day, it just happened. The two had sex. He was so skinny and when he came, Ember threw up. It was horrible. She didn't like to see a guy cum and the fact that he had a puny boy body didn't make it better. It was a disaster.

Ember was kind of lonely sleeping by herself every night in her apartment. She hoped he would stay after they had sex. He laid with her for a little while and then had to go home. He asked her if the sex was really that bad that she had to throw up. She told him she had no idea what made her throw up. They brushed it off and he left. But she knew he wouldn't be just a booty call. Ember knew he liked her a lot, so she wasn't worried. She was also pretty sure he would want to have sex again without her throwing up, to redeem himself.

Keith was skinny but knew how to give it to her. The sex ended up being good after the first time. She knew he would fall in love after having sex with her, so she put in work. They continued hanging out, going to nice places, and having sex. He kept coming over but always had to leave before the next day. She didn't want to question it, though. He said he wanted her to be his girlfriend, but he would rather keep things the way they were without a title. She went with it.

Keith told her he wanted to learn how to drive because he lived in New York and there was never a reason before for him to learn to drive. She taught him how to drive and he got his license. Ember helped him better his life and he made her happy. The holidays came and he said he bought her something nice for Christmas. She went all out and bought him sneakers, boots, and clothes. When they exchanged gifts, he bought her a heart pendant that looked like a little girl's necklace. She was expecting something nicer, but she liked it because it was from him, and it was the thought that counted. She was still mad that she spent more money than he did, though.

On New Year's Eve, he said that he would go over to her apartment but never did. She was kind of hurt that she had to spend it alone. He texted her and asked her if she loved him. She was mad now. She thought, "Why would he dis me and then text me to ask me if I love him?" So, she answered his question by asking him the same question and he said he did love her. He said his mom was really sick and that was why he couldn't make it, but he wanted her to know he loved her. Ember was so happy that he said it but mad that he texted it.

When they hung out the next time, he told her he loved her in person. She looked at him and wanted to say it back but couldn't. How could she love him but not be his girl? So, she just smiled. He told her that she didn't have to say it back until she was ready. He was such a good guy. He met all her friends and her family. Her mom swore he had a girlfriend, but she figured after a year, she would know if he did. Guess again.

Ember was out shopping with her mom one day when Keith called her. She answered, only to find out it wasn't Keith. It was a girl who asked for Ember. Ember said, "Who is this?" She said, "This is Keith's wife." Her jaw dropped. She had to sit down. She felt sick. She said, "He didn't tell you he had a wife and six kids?" Ember quietly said, "No" as she wiped the tears from her eyes. She went on to say, "Yes. We have six kids together and when I gave birth to my sixth child who is not even a year old, he was out with you." Ember asked her why she didn't call her right away when she found out about her. She said he told her they were just friends, and she believed him. Ember couldn't believe it. That was why he didn't want to be her man. That was why he never stayed over until the next day. That was why she was never invited to his house.

Ember told his wife that she would tell her whatever she wanted to know, out of respect for her. After all, Ember was in a much better position than her. She could move on. Ember was single with no kids. His wife had a cheating husband and was trapped with six kids. So, she and Ember talked on the phone for hours and days. She told Ember how he would be rough with her when they had sex, and he was never like that before he met Ember. Ember told her they had sex all the time and that he would take her out. His wife said she felt bad because, if Ember loved him, she didn't want her to be hurt. Ember told her she felt bad because he should've been supporting his children with the money he was using to take Ember out. Everyone seemed to feel bad about what he did except for him.

Keith called Ember and said he was sorry. He said he never thought he would fall in love with her. He never thought it would be that serious when they first met, and he didn't know how to tell her after it went too far. She told him she couldn't be with him or talk to him anymore, even though it broke her heart. She couldn't do that to another woman because she had it done to her and it didn't feel good. He said they weren't legally married, and they were only married because they had lived together for so long. He said they didn't have sex anymore, and he just stayed with her because they had children together. Whatever the reason, he lied, and Ember had to say goodbye.

Ember couldn't lie to herself. It did hurt. He called her after that. She put an icon of the poison symbol that would come up on her phone every time he called. She told his wife that she would find someone else. His wife said, "After you told me everything about the guys you have dated, I am afraid that no matter who else you date, he will be the same guy with a different name." Ember told her she was moving on and hoped they could work things out. She apologized, even though Keith should have been the one telling her he was sorry. That was the last time they spoke despite her attempts to meet up with Ember to see what she looked like. And Ember knew she would eventually move on. Lesson learned. But there was one lingering question: Would Ember really continue to meet the same dude, different name? Or did she have the power to prove her wrong, meet a genuinely good guy, and be happy?

CHAPTER TEN

Two-Timing Todd

One warm summer day, Ember decided to take a bus to New York with her friend, Lisa. Ember got dressed up in a sexy red sun dress and red pumps. They parked her car right near the tunnel to the city, took the bus, and walked around. Ember got a lot of attention, like always, but no men seemed to catch her eye. There was one who said something, and Lisa told Ember that he was cute, but she did not look back for some reason. As it began to get late, they got on a bus back to her car. While they were on the bus, a guy walked on. He looked just like Vincent but a little shorter. He was wearing sunglasses and a shirt that said, "Hoboken Baseball." He sat down behind them. Lisa commented on Ember's hair color, saying that she liked it and Ember responded by saying that it was a mess that day. He chimed in and said that he liked it. Ember turned around and smiled. As they were about to get off the bus, he asked Ember for her name and then her number. She responded and asked him where he was going. He was going to Passaic, which was where Lisa lived, and where they were driving to once they got off the bus. Ember asked him if he wanted a ride there. Both he and Lisa looked at her like she was crazy. Ember thought to herself, "What do I have to lose? I just found out the person I have been dating for over a year is married with six kids- how much worse could it get?"

He began to get off the bus with them and stopped and asked, "Are you sure?" Ember said, "Are you coming or not?" They walked to her car, which was parked at the gym where Tyler worked out. He got in and Ember asked Lisa to drive. They talked and she learned that his name was Todd. He said that he was on his way back from his son's baseball practice, as he was the coach for the team. Ember couldn't help but tell him that she just went out with a guy who had six kids that he failed to tell her about. He said that he would never hide the fact that he has a child. They dropped him off and he said that he would call her.

Later that night, he called Ember while she was still with Lisa. When she answered, he asked her if she wanted to get some drinks with him and his friends. Ember told him that she was busy but thanked him for the offer. She was excited about him wanting to bring her around his friends so soon. Ember asked him what he was doing while they were talking, and he said that he was smoking a blunt. Although this normally would have been a complete turnoff for her, she figured she would let it slide. Ember still wasn't over Keith and needed to hang out to get her mind off things.

The first time they hung out was at her apartment. He brought her a bottle of wine. Her mom and sister were there helping her put up an air conditioner. He quickly took over and put it up himself. Ember realized he was handy. He said he worked in construction. Then, they watched a basketball game on television while he ran his fingers through her hair. Todd told Ember he had a house of his own with a pool and that his mom stayed with him for the time being, as he did not like to be alone. He did mention he didn't drive but was waiting to have his license restored due to parking tickets. Todd said he would always get to Ember, and she would never have to pick him up. Everyone thought he was a good catch. It was such a change since she had gone out with such losers before.

Keith was still calling Ember to apologize and try to get her back. Todd noticed the poison symbol that came up on the screen every time Keith called, and she told him about Keith. They talked that night, and he told her how he had a son but did not have feelings for the mother of his child. He said she was married, and he appreciated how his son was fortunate enough to have two dads. They talked for hours. Ember liked the fact that they hung out a lot and he did not pressure her to have sex. He played it cool. She figured he must really like her. She made him wait three months before she had sex with him.

One night, they planned to go clubbing with her friends. He called her and said he wanted to go but he didn't have any money because his brother was locked up for child support and he had to bail him out. He said he was too embarrassed to go out without money. So, Ember offered to pay. She figured she liked him, and he took her out a few times before that, so it was no big deal. That was the first mistake in this relationship.

Ember and her friend picked him up at his house to go clubbing in New York. That would be mistake number two since he promised she would never have to pick him up. While he was in the car, he flipped out because he thought he had lost his chain. They looked for it and Ember noticed it under her seat. He said it was very expensive and that he was nervous he had lost it. She went to pick it up and figured it was heavy, so she picked it up with force. It ended up being extremely light, and it almost flew out of her hands. Ember and her friend then suspected it was fake but neither said anything. She later confirmed it was fake. He lied about having spent so much money on it (or maybe he thought $20 was a lot of money). Ember looked closer at it when he left it on her dresser another day and saw it was missing stones and the part that was supposed to be gold turned green. There was no way that it was real. This was the first lie she caught him in.

When they got to the club, it was late and the girl at the door said the guest list was dead. She wouldn't let them in. She let Todd in, though, as well as a long line of nasty-looking girls. She was clearly hating. Ember started to say, "If you don't let me in, you will be dead like your list." Instead, she laughed and walked off the line. Todd started arguing with the bouncers and got them in. The two danced together and took pictures with each other. Ember had a lot of fun. Her outfit was trendy yet classy and she looked pretty. When they dropped Todd off, Tyler called her. Ember and her friends met up with Tyler for breakfast. Todd wanted to go to breakfast but she figured she could use Tyler to play hard to get with Todd without either of them knowing. If Tyler hadn't called her, she probably would have gone to breakfast with Todd. She also would have had to pay because he already let her know he had no money. This way, Todd would know he would have to be up on his game. Todd called her to make sure she got home ok, but she didn't answer because she was with Tyler.

The following week, Ember was shopping at the mall when Todd called and said he was near the mall with his son. He asked her if she wanted to meet up so she could meet his son. Ember couldn't believe it. They met up. His son was adorable. His son told her some jokes and they laughed. Then, she dropped his son off and Todd stayed over. They watched the Kung Fu Panda movie, and he began kissing her. One thing led to another, and they had sex. He insisted on using a condom and even brought one with him, which made her feel safe. He slept over. They woke up in the morning and both went to work. On her way to work, he called her. She missed his call because she was driving. He left a message saying he had a wonderful time and that he enjoyed every moment they had together. Ember was sprung. She hadn't been that happy in a very long time.

They continued going out. They would go out with his son on the weekends and alone during the week. He would sleep over sometimes. They went to the pool with his son once and she figured she would offer to pay her way since he had to pay for him and his son. He got mad and told her to put her money away. He added that, as long as he was her man, he would always pay for her. He was the sweetest.

When Ember first met Todd's nephew, he said, "Where is my other titi (aunt)? I like her and her son better. Don't you want to be with her instead?" Ember's heart sank when she heard him say this. She realized he was a little kid and didn't know any better, but it still hurt, and it didn't help that he said it in front of everyone. Ember promised herself that she would be the best girlfriend she could be so that maybe he would change his mind. Looking back, Ember realized she shouldn't have to prove anything to anyone. But, at the time, she thought she had to compete with his ex-girlfriend.

On the anniversary of his dad's death, they visited the cemetery. As they were leaving, he said there was something he needed to tell her. He looked at Ember and began crying. He told her he had lied to her. Ember got nervous and asked what he lied about. Todd said he told her he was 28 years old, but he was really 38. She laughed and told him that wasn't a big deal. He apologized for lying to her. She appreciated the fact that he was man enough to come clean and tell the truth. It made her like him even more. Ember was even happier that he didn't have to tell her anything serious, like he was cheating on her, as the rest of the guys she dated did.

One morning, Todd woke up and asked Ember if she cared about him. She told him that she did. Then, he asked her if she trusted him, and she said she did because he had not given her any reason not to. He went on to explain how he needed $700 to have his driver's license restored. He wanted to know if he could borrow the money and promised he would pay her back. He said that, if he had a license, he would be able to get around faster and it would be a great help, as he would be able to get his son to baseball practice and games and he would be able to continue to coach his son's team. Ember agreed to lend him $700 to reach his goal. She truly believed he would pay her back. When she thought about it, she felt she trusted and cared about him, so it was not a problem for her. He was trying to better his life and Ember wanted to help him.

Ember could never forget the first time Todd ever told her he loved her. They were lying on her couch in her living room, and he said he loved her. He took about a half-hour describing all the reasons why he loved her. He said she was beautiful, smart, and caring. He told her his son loved her, and his family did too. He said he wished he would have met her sooner and that he wanted to be with her for a very long time. Ember was ecstatic and wanted to cry tears of joy. She felt he was the one. If it were up to her at the time, he would have been the last chapter of this book. Instead, he would soon be bumped down to the worst chapter of her life for what he said and did next. He said he was in a relationship with a woman named Megan for six years before he met Ember. He said, although he did not have any kids with her, he was like a father to her fifteen- year-old son, adding that he still had contact with her so that he could keep up to date on how her son was. Ember said she understood even though she wondered why he couldn't contact her son directly since he was grown. He was fifteen years old.

Later that night, Ember noticed Todd's phone was ringing off the hook at 5 am. She reached over him while he was sleeping to see who was calling that many times so early and saw it was Megan. She copied down the phone number and kept it just in case she ever needed it in the future.

The next morning, they got up and Todd was going to drive her to work and use her car to take his son to baseball practice like he always did. When they got into the car, Ember couldn't help but ask him why

Megan would be calling him so many times at 5 am. She clearly could not have to tell him anything about her son at that time. She asked him if he was being completely honest with her, and he said he was. Ember asked him if she knew about her and that he had a girlfriend and he just looked at her and told her he wasn't sure if she knew. Ember told him she was going to call her, and he must have thought Ember didn't have her number and that she was kidding so he said, "Go ahead. Call her." And that is just what Ember did. She took out her phone and began dialing her number. She didn't block her number because she had nothing to hide. That wasn't her style anyway. He looked nervous and surprised as Ember dialed her number. When she picked up the phone, Ember told her who she was. Then, she apologized for getting her involved, but she told her that she was Todd's girlfriend and just wanted to make sure there wasn't anything going on between them before she decided to take things with Todd further. She said, "Oh, you are the one with the red truck?" Ember was at a loss for words. She couldn't believe what she was hearing. She went on to say that he gave her a ride in Ember's truck and told her it was a rental. She said she did not believe it was a rental because she saw women's clothes in the back seat, which made her suspicious. Megan went on to tell Ember that her and Todd break up on and off and she said he just uses Ember for her car and money. She said that he continues to go to her apartment to ask her to be with him and that she did not know anything about Ember being his girlfriend. Ember thanked her for the information and hung up.

Ember turned to Todd and looked at him with tears in her eyes. She asked him how he could do that to her. Todd said that she was "crazy" and that she wasn't over him because he decided to move on, and she was making up stories to break them up because she didn't want him to be happy. Todd went on to say that he gave her son a ride home from baseball practice and he must have told her that Todd was driving Ember's truck, or she must have seen him in it, but he denied that she was ever in it. He hugged Ember and said he would never lie to her, adding that he did not want to lose her. A part of Ember believed Megan because she knew any time a guy says a girl is crazy, it probably isn't true, or the girl is crazy because the guy made her that way. Nate used to say Ember was crazy when the only crazy thing about her was choosing to stay with him at the time after all he did to her. But Ember believed his story more because she wanted to believe him, so she decided to drop the whole thing. It was also too late for her to drop Todd off and still make it to work so she let him use the car that day, as usual.

Todd wanted Ember to have his baby. He said he wanted another child and that she would make a great mother. He made her feel special. One morning, she wasn't feeling well. She thought she could be pregnant, and he was so excited. Ember was scared to get pregnant so when she started feeling sick, she shared her fears with him. He wasn't working at the time, and she had to work two jobs and go to school to support them. He said it would all work out and she told him she really hoped she wasn't pregnant because she needed more time to save money and plan things out. He started crying and said he was disappointed. He began praying, "Dear Lord, if it wasn't meant to be, please let her get her period." As Ember got up to get a tissue to wipe her tears, she realized she had gotten her period. That must have been a sign that it wasn't meant to be. She would have been pregnant with the devil's child. He yelled at her when she told him she got her period and told her to never tell him she thought she was pregnant ever again unless she knew for sure. Then, knowing Ember had an abortion in the past, he called his son in front of her and said, "I love you. I am glad your mom never had an abortion, and we decided to have you." How fucked up was that? Ember knew he wasn't any good for her at that moment. She should have let him go then. But she stayed.

After a while, Ember learned that Todd lied to her more than once. He did not have a house of his own. It was his mother's house. She forgave him because she already had feelings for him. He called her one day and told her that he was laid off from work. Now, all the things that made him different from the rest of the guys that Ember had dated in the past were not true. Todd ended up not working for over a year. He would work somewhere long enough to make money and then collect unemployment and would quit after that. Ember had to climb over him while he was sleeping every morning to work two jobs and go to school. But she dealt with it because she loved him. He was the first guy who stayed with her in her own apartment and, although he never offered to help with rent or groceries, she enjoyed his company. She liked having him and his son around. Todd would sometimes stay over by her apartment and sometimes stay at his mom's. It seemed that the more time passed by and the longer the relationship went on, the more Ember was finding out about lies that Todd had told to impress her and make her fall for him.

Time passed by and everything was back to normal and great. Todd's son would sleep over Ember's apartment. She would make breakfast for them. She would visit his mom's house. She was in love. Halloween came around and they decided that she would be a deviant housewife, and he would be the gardener while her make-believe husband was out of town. She wore a short skirt with an apron that said, "deviant housewife" and had a spatula that said, "My husband is out of town." He wore overalls and a fisherman's hat, and they pinned condoms, a watering can, and a shovel onto his overalls. He really looked like a gardener while her husband was out of town.

They went clubbing that night and everyone loved their creative costumes. Ember happened to see a guy she met while on vacation in the Dominican Republic with her mom and he bought them each a drink at the club. Ember didn't drink so she gave her drink to Todd. He had a few sips because he wasn't a big drinker either. They partied, danced, and had fun. At the end of the night, Ember was tired, so Todd offered to drive them home. They were talking and missed the exit to her apartment, so they had to go another way. As they were driving, there was a cop on the side of the road. He began following them but didn't pull them over until after about two miles of being behind them. The only reason Ember could think of for the officer to pull them over was that Todd was a dark-skinned man wearing a Halloween costume in a white neighborhood. She didn't want to make it a race issue, but it seemed that way.

When he pulled them over, he said it was because Todd was impeding traffic by driving too slowly. Then, he asked them where they were coming from. Ember told him they were coming from a Halloween party. He asked them if they had been drinking, and Todd said he had two beers. She said she did not drink at all. The police officers said they had to do a sobriety test on Todd. They took him out of the car to complete the test. They searched the entire car as well. They asked Ember why she would let him drive if she didn't have anything to drink and she told them it was because he wasn't drunk, and she was tired. They said he passed the breathalyzer, but they were going to take him to the police department anyway.

Ember followed them to the police department. As she was in the lobby, she heard a cop say, "We don't have anything on him. Make him give a urine sample and maybe it will be dirty." Then, she heard the officers yelling at him and telling him to get up to pee. It sounded like he wasn't cooperating. One officer went outside and screamed at Ember, asking what Todd was on. She had no idea what he was talking about. Then, they brought Todd out. His tongue was hanging out of his mouth, his eyes were darting back and forth, and he was strapped down to a stretcher. Ember started to cry and panic. He was just fine when they were in the car and now, he looked crazy. She wondered what could have happened. She thought maybe the guy at the club drugged her drink and then Todd drank it, and it affected him instead. She was shaking and crying. When they got to the hospital, the cop was nasty and yelled at her for letting him drive. He handed Ember tickets for Todd and gave her one for allowing him to drive under the influence. Although the nurse told the officer that he had to stay to get the urine results under the law, he opted to leave. Ember stayed with Todd the whole time.

Ember looked through Todd's phone and called his friend, Curtis. She asked him if he had any idea what Todd could be on, and she told him the story. Curtis said he would go to the hospital. He went to the hospital smelling and looking like death. She asked Curtis again what he thought he was on, and he said it could be a number of things: heroin, crack, PCP, and the list went on. He said, "You didn't know he was a drug addict?" Then, he said, "I better call Megan and let her know he is ok." Ember looked like she saw a ghost. Then, he looked at her and said, "Just kidding. Lighten up."

The nurses did tests. One nurse woke him up and said, "Do you smoke weed?" He turned around and said,

"No." The nurse said, "No? Well, I know you smoke weed, and someone must have laced your weed with angel dust because your drug test came back positive for PCP." Ember almost dropped to the floor. Then, Curtis said to Todd, "Remember when our friend Moses smoked and ended up in the hospital?" I am going to tape you and put it online. They thought it was a joke, but Ember knew it was anything but a joke. She was ready to leave the hospital because she needed sleep. As she was leaving, Curtis said, "Nice ass. I would fuck you." Ember was so angry and replied, "You would never get the chance, nasty bitch."

Ember went home and Todd came by later. Her friend Lisa was also at her apartment. He kept saying someone must have drugged his drink. Lisa took over and threw him out of Ember's apartment. She gathered all his things and told him he had to leave. Ember wanted to seem tough, so she went along with it even though she wanted him to stay. He laid down and said, "Let's watch a movie. I don't want to leave you. It's not my fault." Lisa made him get up and he went home.

The day after Halloween, Ember called Todd, and his son picked up the phone. She asked him if she could talk to Todd. His son did not know what to say and could not tell her where Todd was. She needed to talk to him because she realized Curtis had taken her driver's license the night before at the hospital. She called Todd over and over, figuring he may be at his best friend Rebecca's house. His son told Ember they were not at Rebecca's, they were in New York. She went online and saw pictures of Todd and three girls. He was kissing one of the girls. This was one day after everything happened at the hospital. She couldn't believe it. He could care less about what she was going through because of him. When she finally got to talk to him, she told him what Curtis said to her at the hospital, and he said he didn't believe her. When she asked him where he was and who those girls in the pictures were, he told her he took his son to a Halloween party, as his son really wanted to go to a party. He called Curtis and Ember went to pick up her license. She was devastated. How could he go out and hang out when she was home hurt because of him? How could he say his son wanted to go to a Halloween party when it was clearly a party at night for adults, and his son should not have been there in the first place?

After she begged him to tell her the truth about what happened on Halloween, Todd later explained to her that he had a blunt of dust with him the night they were pulled over. He did not want to get her into trouble, so he swallowed the blunt while the cops searched the car. This is why he had to be carried out on a stretcher once the effects hit him.

This is also why Ember had no idea what was going on, as he was fine when he was driving. He could have ruined Ember's life. She could have been arrested if the cops would have found the drugs. However, he saw it like he got her out of trouble. He did not see that he did anything wrong. This should have been enough for her to break up with him, but she didn't. Since she received a ticket that night, Todd said he would do anything he had to so it would be dismissed. Ember stayed with him until the court date almost a year later because she wanted to make sure he would plead guilty so her ticket would be dismissed. If he didn't, she would have a charge equivalent to a DWI and would lose her license and probably her job. He kept praising himself, saying how he was helping her when, in reality, she would have never been in that situation if it weren't for him. Ember also stayed with him and hoped he would get the help he needed. He was addicted to PCP and that was serious, but Ember figured he would get help since he later admitted he needed it. Since she stayed with him and played it cool for a year instead of cutting him off, the relationship dragged on. It was the worst thing that she could've done. She also had to pay $7,000 in attorney fees to fix the situation.

After Halloween, he came back, apologized again, and said that his son wanted to make a pizza from scratch. They got all the ingredients and began making the pizza. Todd didn't help at all. He said he was going downstairs for a walk. When he didn't return for over two hours, Ember went downstairs to look for him only to find him being dropped off in front of her apartment by a girl in a car. Ember flipped out on him and started screaming. He said it was just a friend. She asked him what her name was, and he said her name was Rox. She said, "Yeah. Because she looks like she smokes crack rocks." Ember was fuming. He said he was sick of her always blaming him for everything. Ember screamed at him again, as she remembered Megan mentioning that he had a girl named Rox. It must have been her. He turned around as she was screaming, spit in her face, and walked away. As he walked away, he said he never loved her, that he didn't even like her, and that he was, in fact, only using her. Ember told him she was going to call the police. He said, "Go ahead. I didn't do anything except blow air in your face." He had spit in her face and was trying to tell her he didn't. Ember wasn't sure whether the gaslighting and mental abuse were worse than the fact that he spit in her face, but all of it made her feel as though her life was over.

Sometimes during their relationship, Ember became suspicious of what he was doing. She watched him dial his voicemail code one night and got the code. Later that week, he told her he was going to go to New York with a friend. She checked his voicemail, and it was a girl named Vanessa saying she couldn't wait to see him. Ember confronted him and he changed his voicemail code immediately. He denied it, of course, saying that she was going to help him study for his GED since she was a teacher. When he visited Ember later that day, Ember made him call Vanessa. He refused and said he did not want to bother her. Ember said she didn't care and told him she was going to break up with him if he did not call her. So, he called her. The conversation went like this: She picked up and said, "What are you doing? Why didn't you come by?" He said, "I was at my grandmother's house in New York." She replied, "How could you be around New York and not come see me?" He said, "Ok. I will let you go." Before he could hang up, she said, "How is your little girlfriend? Is that why you didn't come over?" He hung up and Ember asked why she would say that, and he said he didn't know but that Ember should be happy she knew he had a girlfriend. Again, Ember was hurt.

When Ember first found out Todd cheated, she wanted to work harder to make him continue to love her and she did whatever it took to show him she was better than anyone else he was ever with. The thing is she didn't realize there was nothing she could do to prove this. Ember knew she was the best thing that ever happened to him. She knew she could do better. She just had to accept that it didn't matter what he thought. She had to believe it. He didn't cheat on her because of her. He cheated on her because he was a cheater, and she couldn't make him faithful. He was going to cheat even if she bought him things, spent time with him, had sex with him ten times a day, and looked sexy all the time. It didn't matter because, just like her relationship with her dad, it wasn't about her, it was about him.

Once Ember realized this, she became angry, so she began cheating on him to let him know how it felt. The difference was he never looked through her phone or questioned her, so he never found out. She would tell him about guys who hit on her and offered to take her out or even about guys she cheated on him with, but he didn't care. Either he didn't believe her, or he didn't like her enough to care. She even posted a picture of her and Tyler hugging in a club. He saw it and could care less, even though Tyler looked better than him. Ember found that the more she would get mad at Todd, the more other guys would benefit because she would have sex with guys she normally would not give the time of day to, just to get back at him. In the long run, not only was Todd hurting her, but she was also hurting herself.

A few days later, Ember found a note in Todd's bookbag to his friend Curtis who was locked up. It read, "I am still with Vanessa, the school teacher, Rebecca, and Rox but I keep my girl around as the main one. I am following your footsteps." There was a picture of Todd and a huge, nasty stripper and on the back of the picture it said, "Rox." She was missing teeth. Ember looked at the date on the back of the picture and it was the month before. There was also a picture of Vanessa who looked like a man with a wig on. It was a picture taken in his mom's backyard. Ember realized he brought other women around his family and his son when she couldn't be there because she was busy working, just as Megan said he did. Ember wasn't special. She knew he was cheating. She had proof. As embarrassing as it was, she kept thinking he loved her and couldn't let go.

Another time when Ember checked his phone, she saw he had hung out with a girl, and she had texted him saying it was nice seeing him. He wrote back to her saying he missed her. Ember called her and she said she was his first girlfriend. She said she was married but found Todd online and hung out with him. She then asked Ember how long she and Todd were together. Ember told her they were together for three years. She said, "He obviously doesn't love or respect you if he hasn't proposed or made future plans with you." Her words hit Ember hard. She wanted to be mad, but she couldn't. She was right. He was taking her as a joke. Ember shouldn't have needed her to tell her that, but she never really thought about it. Ember was living off of fantasies that things would go back to the way they were in the beginning. They never did. The beginning was like a job interview for Todd where he put up a front to be someone he never was. When she found out who he really was and that he was nothing like who he portrayed himself to be, it was too late because she fell in love with who he pretended to be.

Ember once had her friend Jessica prank call Todd and tell him she was someone he met at a club. She called him and the conversation went like this: Jessica: "Hey, Todd. This is Jan. I met you on Main Avenue in Passaic a few weeks ago. What are you up to tonight? Do you want to hang out?" Todd: "I don't remember who you are. Do you want to meet up for a minute?" Jessica: "Sure. I live on Madison. Can you get here?" Todd: "Yeah. I am on my way now." They actually heard him getting into a taxi so Jessica said, "Are you getting into a taxi because I only date guys who drive." He replied, "I drive but my car is in the shop. I am taking a taxi." She got another call and told him to hold on. When she got back to the line about three minutes later, he was still holding. She told him that was just her baby daddy on the other line, and they were fighting. He didn't say anything about it. Then, she said, "Do you have your own apartment?" He told her he owned a house. She said, "Then maybe we should meet at your house because I have a lot of pests in my apartment." Todd said, "Don't worry. I like pets. What kind do you have?" She said, "No, pests. I have a variety and I am afraid one might jump up and bite you in the thigh." Ember and Jessica started laughing and she hung up. It wasn't really funny, though. Ember learned a lot from prank calling him, especially how he lies and tries to act charming when he meets a new person, which is exactly what he did with Ember in the beginning.

Todd usually had his son every weekend. If he wanted to go out, he would either have his son stay at his mom's house or at his best friend Rebecca's house. Ember met Rebecca. She was as skinny as a stick and looked sick. She was by no means pretty. She had six kids and Todd's son used to play with them. Ember found it a little strange that she used to do everything for him, including his laundry. He told Ember that Rebecca gave him pedicures even though she thought he had the ugliest, crustiest feet ever. Ember asked him if he ever got with her and he said they were just friends and that he would never get with her, as he had standards.

On Todd's birthday the year before, Ember got his family together for some cake. She had a special cake made for him with a Kung Fu Panda theme since that was the movie they were watching when they first made their relationship official. She even got his sister, who didn't talk to him much, to come. It was great. She went all out to have all his friends sign a huge poster with their picture on it and she gave it to him that night. Ember went out of her way to make his day special. At the end of the night, Todd made her stop by Rebecca's to bring her the rest of the cake, without even asking Ember if it was okay. Ember was so upset. She let it happen because she wanted to be a great girlfriend but deep down inside, she felt like an idiot. Ember worked so hard to make him happy and he turned around and made Rebecca happy.

There were other times that Ember felt like this. She went on vacation with her family. When she would call Todd from vacation, he didn't pick up. When he did pick up, the phone would hang up. He said he was at Coney Island with his son and did not have reception. Ember's bill was $550 while she was there, and she barely got to talk to him. When she got back from vacation, she gave him a bottle of his and Rebecca's favorite liquor. She didn't like Rebecca but realized she had to accept that she was his best friend. Ember offered to hang out with Rebecca and share it with Rebecca and Todd. She figured they could hang out and she could get to know her. Todd took it upon himself to give the bottle of liquor to Rebecca. When Ember found out, she was furious. His excuse was that he thought Ember said they could drink it together. Ember did say that, but with her there too. She was heartbroken but he reassured her that he didn't do it on purpose. Ember felt like he made her look like a complete loser. She figured she was suspicious and believed anything was possible because of what happened with Nate in the past. She let it go but the thought was always in the back of her mind.

    Todd's birthday was in January and Ember's was in February. Although she did all the things she did for his birthday because she wanted to, Ember figured she could expect him to surprise her for her birthday. He gave her a surprise, alright. Megan called Ember that day and said he had been to her apartment the night before and they had sex, and she wanted to make sure they weren't together anymore. Ember couldn't believe it. She thought, "How could he do this to me?" Megan went on to tell her everything Ember already knew but was in denial about and some things she could have never imagined. She told Ember she suspected Todd had sex with Rebecca while he was with her, but she couldn't prove it. She told her that she should never feel special when Todd brings her around his son and family, as he does that with every woman he meets to get them to like him more. She told her Todd used her for things such as her car and money. She told her he still talked to his exes, including her. Ember asked her if she ever had a bacteria problem from having sex with him, as she kept getting infections. She said she did, adding that her doctor yelled at her, telling her not to return to his office because, although it was not an STD, it was bacteria that he was spreading by having sex with multiple partners and by not using a condom. Ember couldn't believe it. Megan knew about everything bad that was happening to Ember because of him. Megan accused him of getting with this older woman whom she referred to as a "grandma" and who she believed had an STD. She said she even went to court with him in the past because she was afraid he had an STD, and she filed a restraining order. She said she had sex with him then because he brought his STD test results to her, proving he was negative. She told Ember she was at Coney Island with him and his son while Ember was on vacation. She told Ember he never paid any of her bills despite telling Ember he supported Megan financially when they were together. She let Ember know that he told her he loved her and wanted to get back with her and start a family. By the time they hung up, Ember wanted to die.

When Todd came over that night for Ember's birthday, she told him she talked to Megan and let him know everything she had told her. She asked him about the girl Megan said he had gotten with who had an STD. Todd said that was outrageous. He called the girl, and she said she was only friends with Todd. She said she did not have an STD, that Megan was crazy, and what she was saying was defamation of character. The girl said she took Megan to court for this and showed her results were negative. Todd also showed Ember his negative test results. Ember couldn't believe that Megan would lie about something that serious. She thought maybe she was that crazy. Ember asked Todd how he could do this on her birthday. How could he go to see her? His response was, "It's your birthday?" She told him to leave and that it was over. It was the worst birthday she ever had. The feeling inside of her was more than words could explain and the worst part of it all was that when she told him it was over, he didn't do anything to convince her to stay with him. He just left, probably to be with Megan.

Shortly after Ember spoke to Megan, she was at the baseball field watching Todd's son's game when Megan showed up with her friend. Ember knew it was her because she had seen a picture of her online before. Her friend came up to Todd and started talking to him. He said, "Don't be rude. Say hello to my girlfriend." She gave Ember a nasty look and said, "Oh, hi." Ember ignored her since she gave her an attitude. Then, her friend walked near Megan and screamed out, in the middle of the baseball field full of kids and parents, "You're an ugly bitch." Todd's guy friend, who went out with Megan's friend before, called Todd over to talk to them. Ember warned Todd that if he went over there, it would be over. He stayed near Ember. She wasn't going to fight her back or call her names because she had more respect for herself. Megan screamed out, "You shouldn't have invited me to the game if you were going to be here with her." Ember wondered: Did he really invite her? Was she that crazy? Or was he? Todd's son came over to Ember after the game and said, "Don't worry about her. She is like a sumo wrestler, and you are a diva." Ember loved Todd's son. She used that as another reason to stay with Todd. After all, his son was right. She did look beautiful that day and she was a lady whereas his ex was a hot mess.

Ember remembered Todd telling her that his ex used to wear three bras because she was flat-chested. She was wearing a low-cut shirt that day. So, Ember turned around, looked at her chest, and said, "Nice back." Megan was ready to hit her as she walked away with Todd and his son. Ember would later find out that instead of fighting her, she should've listened to her, as she was right about everything that she told her.

A few weeks later, Ember received a call from Rebecca. She said she had heard what happened between Todd and Ember and she wanted to tell her that Megan was crazy. She told Ember that she never got with Todd. Todd also had Ember talk to his seven-year-old son who reassured her they were not with Megan at Coney Island and that it was only Todd and his son. Todd told Ember that Megan made up the whole thing because Ember brought everything up when she called her, so Megan went along with it. He told Ember that Megan was jealous and that is why she said Todd was using her. He told Ember the only reason she called her was because Ember called her first and she had Ember's number. He said Megan was trying to break them up, probably because she missed him. So, being in denial, once again, Ember decided to believe him. After all, he would not have his son lie and have Rebecca go through all the trouble to call her and lie, would he? So, she got back with him. She even forgave him for forgetting her birthday.

During the time they weren't together, her friend Joey who was a police officer told her that Todd was involved in a car accident with a car his mom had bought him that Ember didn't even know about. He said that the car crashed, and a girl was in the driver's seat with glass from the windshield all over her. When Ember asked what she looked like, he described Rebecca, adding that she looked like a "space cadet." Joey said he went up to Rebecca and she said she had taken Todd's car without his permission, and she didn't want him to know. As she was talking to the police, Todd started running down the street and screaming at her. The cops told him he would be arrested if he didn't calm down and Joey said he looked like he wanted to hit her. Joey said they didn't arrest him because he knew Ember. Ember told him they should have arrested him. It could have been her car and she was thankful it wasn't. The two were losers. Ember kept thinking they were both drug addicts and probably did sleep together. She told Joey that there had to be more to that story because Rebecca would never take his car without him knowing. She was always doing everything he said, like his little puppet.

The next time Ember saw Todd, she asked him about this. He was mad that she even knew about it. He said he was high and crashed his car while Rebecca was in the passenger seat. When he crashed, he left Rebecca in the car and fled. When he came back, he was so high that he didn't remember he crashed the car and thought Rebecca did it. He told Ember to thank her friend for not arresting them. Rebecca ended up going to court and taking the blame. Ember thought to herself, "I wouldn't even do that. There had to be something more to their relationship."

For the next two years, her life was a living hell. She would pay not only to go out with Todd but also for his son. She never once got a Christmas gift, a birthday gift, or was taken out anywhere. Todd even stopped bringing her around his family and friends unless he just needed a ride from her to get somewhere. He didn't work and she worked two jobs and went to school. She had a lot of bills, and he added to them without any remorse. She would drive him and his son everywhere. She helped his son with his homework. Todd would post pictures online of everywhere they went with his son but would just say it was him and his son, adding what a good father he was. No one ever knew Ember was the one behind the scenes making everything happen by driving them everywhere and paying for everything.

Ember bought his son a birthday gift once and he didn't like it, so Todd agreed to return it and pay the difference for whatever else he wanted. When they got to the register, Todd put his hand in his pocket as if he was going to pay and then walked outside to make a phone call instead. Ember didn't want to hold up the line and she couldn't stand his son looking at her and waiting for his toy, so she paid. Todd never paid her back. And this happened more than once. His hand would always go into his pocket but never come out. He would say he was going to pay but he never helped her with anything, which made her feel horrible, especially because he told her that he used to buy Megan everything and Megan told her that Todd was just using Ember. Ember thought to herself, "Did he ever love me more? Did he even love me at all? Was he using me?"

The arguments went on and on. Ember found out he was always at strip clubs with his friends, including Curtis who was a major loser and tried to have sex with Ember in the past. He began living a single life. Or maybe he was living a single life the whole time and she just refused to notice it. She played him out just to make herself feel better and to make him jealous and mad, but he didn't seem to care. It only made her feel worse. He would never tell her she was pretty anymore. He would never care if other guys tried to kick it while he was with her. It was like she didn't even exist. This went on for a long time. He would leave for days and then come back. When Ember thought she had had enough, she would tell him she wanted to break up with him. He took her as a joke because she would constantly break up with him and then take him back. He had some kind of hold on her and he knew it.

Ember would sometimes confide in her sister's boyfriend and tell him how much it hurt to leave him and how lonely she was when he was gone but how much she knew she should not be with him. Her sister's boyfriend told her to "put down the crack pipe." He was right. But it was easier said than done. Todd was addicted to drugs, but Ember was as addicted to him as much as he was addicted to PCP. Enough was enough. It was time for her to begin her own recovery.

They were broken up for about a month when her bell rang at six in the morning. It was Todd. He said he needed somewhere to stay. Ember told him he could not stay with her. He said they could be roommates, and he wouldn't have any other girls over. Then, he asked her if she had a condom so they could have sex. She told him she didn't need any favors. So, he got up and left and said, "That's why you're single." Ember looked at him dead in his face and said, "That's why you're homeless." He walked down the stairs and then came back up after a minute. She thought he was going to apologize. He only came back because he had forgotten his hat. He took his hat and left again. Ember got ready and went to school that morning. She was miserable, thinking, "Why would he come over to make me feel bad?" She later looked online and saw pictures of him taking his son to a car show like nothing happened. How could he be so cold?

A few months went by, and Ember missed him even though he had done so many terrible things to her. She was busy working two jobs and attending two schools to better her life, so she did not have much time to meet anyone new. Ember was on her way back from school one night when she read an email from Todd that said he missed her and wanted to see her. She answered back three days later, and they made plans to see each other. Ember put on her best outfit, and he came over. He said he was a changed man, and he could not stand to be without her.

This time, she did not believe him. Ember had time to be by herself and take care of her. She went through Todd's Facebook page that night and found her ex-boyfriend, Joseph's, cousin as his friend. As she looked through her page, Ember came across pictures of Joseph on his wedding day. It also said he graduated and was a dentist. She took a deep breath and thought to herself, "He has everything he set out to get in life- a career, a house, and a wife." The only difference is the wife was now the one who would be swimming in the heart-shaped pool instead of her. Ember thought she had replaced him, but it ended up that she was replaced. It seemed he moved on for the better, and she was moving backwards for the worst. She felt like shit.

When Ember mentioned to her sister that she came across Joseph's Facebook page, she said she had to tell Ember something. Her sister told her that she had sex with a guy the same day Ember first had sex with Joseph. Her guy put their condom on top of the garbage can and their mom found it, blaming Ember. It was just a coincidence, and no one would have suspected it was her sister, as she was much younger than Ember was. No one would have ever suspected she was having sex at twelve years old. Ember's heart dropped when she received this news. She had blamed Joseph for not throwing the condom away far from their mom's house and he was telling the truth when he said he did. Ember broke up with him because of this condom only to find out years later it wasn't even their condom that made her mom hate him! What bad luck she had! Here she was getting played out and humiliated, just as Joseph warned would happen when she cheated on him with Nate. Would she ever find true love? She thought, "Why me? Why do all the guys I ever meet start off nice and then end up being liars, cheaters, abusers, and losers?"

Ember knew she needed to get rid of Todd and she continued to look though his page and phone only to find emails to about thirty other girls. He emailed them the same thing he had emailed her. Ember was the only idiot who answered and agreed to meet up with him. He was probably high when he sent the emails. So, she sat him down and asked him to be completely honest with her. He said there was nothing he was hiding and there wasn't anyone else he wanted to be with. Ember figured she had to get more creative to find out the truth. She then said, "I'm surprised none of Rebecca's kids are yours." And he said, "None of them look like me." Ember asked, "How could one look like you if you never had sex with her? Why would that even cross your mind?" He looked at her with this look she would never forget. He had just basically told her that he had sex with Rebecca, and he couldn't take it back. Of course, he tried to cover it up, but she wasn't trying to hear it. He explained they had sex a long time ago and that she was talking to too many guys at the time and he got jealous so they became best friends. He said this was when she was pretty. Ember couldn't even cry. She was mad at herself for believing him when he swore it wasn't true. They both made Ember look stupid. And how could he have been jealous of other guys with her but didn't care who Ember talked to? He must have never really liked Ember.

After years of hard work and sleepless nights, the day finally came when Ember bought her own home. It was the proudest day of her life. The week before, Todd told her he was going out with his friend, claiming it was a friend she had never met. He told her they were just going to a local bar. She figured they would be going to their usual strip club to spend money on strippers instead of helping Ember out with bills or buying her something nice. Or better yet, buying his son something. Ember felt suspicious so she called him, and he didn't answer. She knew his voicemail code, so she checked his messages and found out that he was going out with Curtis, the friend she hated. She pressed "5" and got Curtis's number just in case. She called her friend Lisa, and they decided to go to Passaic to the bar where they said they would be. They weren't there. Curtis's car was parked outside the strip club. When Lisa and Ember went into the club, they weren't there. When they got back outside, his car was gone. So, Ember had Lisa call Curtis's phone and pretend she was a girl they had just met. The conversation went like this: Lisa: "Hi, Curtis?" Curtis: "Yea? Who dis?" Lisa: "It's Bianca. I was the girl who was talking to Todd, and he gave me your number because he said his phone was going to die. Me and my friend want to meet up with you guys." Curtis: "Oh, hey. Exactly which girl were you? Todd talked to a few tonight." Lisa: "I was the prettiest one." Curtis: "Ok. Do you want to meet us at Banana King?" Lisa: "Sure. We will be there in a few minutes." Lisa and Ember drove past Banana King only to find Todd inside kicking it to bitches. They made sure they didn't see them. After they didn't show up, Curtis called Lisa's phone and said that Todd had to leave to go see his girlfriend. Meanwhile, he didn't pick up any of Ember's calls. Ember was right across the street watching him as his phone rang with her number and he continued to talk to bitches. So, they followed him home. Ember met him in front of his mother's house. When Curtis saw them, he came up to the car and said, "So, you're Bianca?" They were caught. Ember told Todd she wanted to check his phone, and he told her that she couldn't. She grabbed his phone and saw that he had been texting a number saved under the name Dave saying he was going to go to her house at 2 am. The texting ended when he said he couldn't make it and she wrote, "I love you." He wrote back, "I loovvveee you too." When Ember asked him whose number that was, he said it was a girl from Florida who he got into a car crash with. She was in New Jersey and wanted to see him. He added that he told her he loved her because he felt bad because her face was deformed after he got into the crash with her. Ember already knew who he was talking about because she had dealt with her before on Facebook and her face was not deformed like he claimed it was. Ember had him call her in front of her. So, he called, and she said she wasn't going to deal with issues he was having with Ember. She said, "Handle your girlfriend and then call me."

The next day, he called Ember, but she didn't pick up. He must have dialed her number by mistake because he left her a voicemail while apologizing to the other bitch on the other line. Ember heard the whole thing. When he called her back later, Ember asked him how he could have the audacity to call her first and apologize to her when it was Ember he should've been begging for forgiveness.

She moved into her new house the following week. Ember loved it and saw it as a way to get away from him and start fresh. She was getting quotes on painting jobs when he called her a few weeks later. He said he could help her paint and get things done. Ember figured she would let him. After all, he did know how to paint and do construction work, and he owed her at least that. He painted her whole house. It came out beautiful, and she didn't have to pay a dime. The only downside was he began staying over at her house.

He would smoke cigarettes, and her house started to smell. He would eat all her food. Ember told him he couldn't move in, so he kept his room in a rooming house that he had on his own and stayed at her house most of the time, not contributing to anything. She was working two jobs and barely making it. Her part-time job as a waitress was slow. She would sometimes make $20 after a seven-hour shift and come home upset, exhausted, and ready to go to sleep only to find him watching television and making a mess. Her house would smell like weed and cigarettes even though she hated smoke and never did anything illegal in her life. She would have to jump over him in the morning and deal with the television blasting while she was trying to sleep. He would not work and did not care that she was suffering just to get by. Then, when she would complain and tell him to keep it down because she was tired, he would ask her why she was so tired. Maybe because she worked hard day in and day out and went to school just to survive? The dust must have clouded his thinking. He didn't have a clue. What kind of man would allow his woman to struggle and sit there and take advantage of her? A loser who knows he can get away with it. He would tell all his friends and everyone in the neighborhood it was "their house" even though he never contributed anything other than painting.

One morning, as she was getting ready for work, he asked her to drive him home to get some things and then pick him up again and bring him back to her house. She flipped out on him and told him she wouldn't drive him around, as she was not a chauffeur. He replied by saying, "I buy you food and take care of you. I have been good and haven't cheated on you in a long time." Was he kidding? Ember thought a camera man was going to pop out and say, "You are on candid camera." He couldn't be serious. A 99-cent hamburger and a small coke that he once bought her wasn't anything he should be bragging about after she supported his lazy ass for years. When he said that, it made her remember one winter when he left her broke, depressed, and alone to go and get high and go to strip clubs. She decided to shovel out her car after a snowstorm when she met a guy in a Range Rover. He asked her where she was going, and she told him she was shoveling out her car to go food shopping. He said he would go with her. He went with Ember, paid for all of her food, and gave her $100. A complete stranger did more for her in one minute without her having to give him anything in return than Todd ever did for her the whole time they were together. Of course, the guy later called her and asked her if he could come over. Ember told him he could at first. Then, she called him back and said, "The snow must have clouded my brain because I don't ever let strangers come over. I am thankful for the fact that you took me food shopping and gave me money. That was very nice of you." That was that. She never heard from him again. And now, Todd was trying to tell her that he supported her and bought her food? It must have been some kind of joke, or he must have smoked so much that he had gone insane.

After he painted, Ember realized it would have been much cheaper to hire someone. Even though most quotes were $2,500 and up, she would've saved by not having to go through him being there for free. She could have paid and been alone. He could care less that Ember had just bought a house and wanted to enjoy it. He saw it as his meal ticket and wanted to stay in it as long as he could. He would stay there all day and do nothing other than play video games, eat, watch television, and say he was looking for work. Ember realized she had to get rid of him or he was going to drive her into the ground. She felt like she owed him something for him helping her fix up the house. She didn't owe him anything but, because of issues with her dad and the way she was brought up, it just felt like she did. He didn't believe Ember when she would tell him it was over- probably because she would say it but never followed her words up with actions. He threatened to mess up her house if she kicked him out. After a while, Ember didn't care. He had to go. She had to finally enjoy what she had worked so hard for on her own.

After all the things he had done to hurt her, she was just tired of him. The day Ember left was not because of anything in particular. It was because she was fed up. She needed some soul-searching and wanted him out of her life. Even though he had done a million things before and she stayed with him, and he was behaving at the time, she left him. She realized that she was trying to change him and make him a better person. She was trying to mold him into who he portrayed himself to be at the beginning of their relationship. She was trying to believe that he would change and go back to being that caring person. Instead, Ember realized he was changing her. He had put her through so much hurt and pain. If she hadn't gained the strength to finally let go, he may have ruined her life forever. She also realized that loving someone shouldn't hurt and love is no excuse to stay in an abusive relationship. Ember was giving her all, and he was giving everything to everyone else. She found herself in a similar situation to when she broke up with Nate. Even though she said she would never be in another abusive relationship time and time again, Todd ended up being just like Nate and the rest of the guys Ember dated, the same dude, different name. She not only had to get rid of Todd, but also had to figure out why she kept getting in the same situation over and over again, and try to stop the vicious cycle.

One day, she just told him to get out and that she never wanted to see him again. He replied, "Really? Are you serious? Over nothing? This is what I get for treating you good and not playing you out?" She said, "Yes. I am serious." Although she thought that would be the worst feeling in the world, it turned out to be the best day of her life. Ember broke up with him once and for all. She knew deep down inside that she deserved better. She was ready to learn from her mistakes and grow, no matter how much it would hurt. She had spent her twenties on dumbass dudes and refused to continue and be like Megan who was forty years old dating losers like Todd. As he walked out, he said, "I hope you aren't afraid of karma because you are going to be lonely and suffer for breaking up with me over nothing." Ember smiled and said, "I am not afraid of karma at all. Karma is what is going on right now." It had to be karma. He took her for granted for so long and abused her and she finally got the strength to let go and say enough is enough. She felt like a new person. Call it karma or call it whatever you want but this was the end of her dating the same dude, different name and the beginning of her being happy with herself before finding the right MAN for the rest of her life.

Shortly after Ember broke up with Todd, she opened a Chinese fortune cookie and her fortune read, "No one can walk backwards into the future." It was so true. She related this to her past. She would have to move on from it to have a future. The thought often crossed her mind to call Todd or Tyler or other guys from her past when she was lonely or upset. Sometimes, it even still does. But when it does, she looks at that fortune that she keeps in her wallet and the thought passes. It just isn't worth it.

CHAPTER ELEVEN

Slim Pickings

This chapter is dedicated to the reason why women would rather be single than go out with one of these dumbass dudes....

Imagine each of the following scenarios:

Scenario Number One: You go out to dinner with your friends one night. As you leave the restaurant and walk to the car, you decide to play around with people who are walking by. Every time you see a guy who looks like your friend's type, you scream out, "She likes you." Then, you all laugh, and your friend turns red. It was funny until it was their turn to play around with you. They see a guy who looks like your type. He is tall and handsome. When your friends tell him you like him, he says, "I like her too." He asks for your number, and you give it to him.

Later that day, he calls you and you begin talking. He asks you what kind of car you drive. Even though you find this question strange, you tell him and then ask him what he drives. He says, "Oh, I get around on my two feets." As the conversation goes on, he asks you where you work. You tell him you are a GED instructor in prison. By telling him that, you figure you could find out two things: if he had ever been to prison and if he had a GED. Sure enough, your plan works. He says, "I have been to prison, but I don't have my GED." "Maybe you can help me get it," he adds. As if that isn't enough for you to end the conversation, he adds, "A lot of girls around here like to have phone sex. Do you want to try it?" You say, "Sure"….pause…"Fuck you!" and hang up. A few seconds later, he calls back and said, "We got disconnected just as the conversation got good." Obviously, he doesn't make it past the first conversation, but he does make for great laughs with your friends.

Scenario Number Two: One night, while clubbing, a guy comes up to you and asks your name. His breath almost kills you. You tell him your name just to be nice. Then, you asked his name. When he says his name is Friday, you can't help but whisper to your friend, "Is that because that is the only day you brush your teeth?" Too bad it was Monday when you met him.

Scenario Number Three: Another night, you go clubbing with your friends and wear a sexy red dress with red heels and red lipstick. You have a tan, which makes your blonde hair look brighter. You can get any guy in the club. This guy who is cute and tall comes up to you and you both start dancing. You end up giving him your number. He calls you a few days later and asks you out on a date. You get ready for your date, and he picks you up. You are excited because he is driving, has a car, and is taking you out.

When you get to the club, he asks what you want to drink. You tell him you want a rum and coke. He says, "No. You are getting a Long Island Iced Tea." It is your first time having that strong of a drink, and you are drunk halfway through it. You dance and he offers to hold your ID and handbag, so you let him. After dancing, you decide to leave. When you get to his car, he tries to make out with you. You are drunk and kick your foot from the passenger seat to the driver's seat to make him stop touching you. He pulls your shoe off and says, "Step on it." You scream and say, "You step on it and drive me home." Before you can pull your foot back, within seconds, he is jerking off with your foot. Thankfully, you get him to stop, and he drives you home.

Scenario Number Four: You met a guy at a club one night. He is the sexiest guy there. You exchange numbers and begin talking. You date for almost a year and you like him. However, you never really hang out. One day, he invites you over to his apartment. It is a great apartment uptown in New York City. He had a white carpet with red walls and black furniture. You love the fact that he has his own apartment. You watch television and hang out. You really like him and are so happy to be hanging out with him. He pulls you on top of him on his couch and you begin kissing. You are about to go further when you look over and see a card that reads, "Baby, we have been together for seven years and I still love you...." You can't read any further. Near the card are kids' toys. He is obviously in a relationship and has kids, which are two things he forgot to mention. So, you jump off of him, get up, and say, "I have to go." You never see him again. However, you are happy he wasn't smart enough to hide those things. His stupidity saved you the pain of really liking him and not knowing he was unavailable to you.

Scenario Number Five: While walking with a friend from school, a sheriff's officer stops you. You think you did something wrong. He just wants to tell you that you are beautiful. You don't think he is cute, but your friend encourages you to give him your number when he asks for it, so you do. He texts you three weeks later, and the conversation goes like this: Him: "Hey, how are you?" You: "I'm good. Who is this (forgetting you even gave him your number)?" Him: "The cop you met the other day." You: "Hey, what's up?" (thinking to yourself-you're not a cop, you're a sheriff's officer and it wasn't the other day-it was three weeks ago). Him: "Send me some pictures." You: Send him a picture of yourself even though you usually don't like doing that (your friend talks you into it because she wants to see if he has any friends for her). Him: "Nice, baby. But send me a sexy picture, a naked one." You: "I'm nobody's baby, bitch. And I guess you are a pig in more ways than one." Him: Must have gotten scared because he hasn't answered back yet.

Scenario Number Six: You are at a diner when you meet a new guy. He is with a famous rapper. You don't pay the rapper much attention because he looks stuck up, but his friend seems cool and is cute. You talk for a while, and end up going out one night after you meet.

When you meet him at the place where you are going, he is drunk, which is a huge turnoff. He begins singing and it turns out that he has a great voice. It isn't great enough to continue talking to him, as it seems he is a drunk who just wants to have sex. He keeps asking you to go back to his apartment and he is acting stupid because he is drunk, so you leave. You erase his number from your phone and don't plan on talking to him ever again.

Years later, you sign up on a dating website and receive a message. You don't realize it at first. But when you exchange numbers and speak to the guy over the phone, you immediately recognize his voice. You know it is him. He sounds like he grew up a little throughout the years, so you continue talking to him. You hang out both alone and with friends. He sends you songs he wrote and sings to you on your voicemail. You fall in love with his voice.

On New Year's Eve that year, you hang out and get tipsy. You and he go to his friend's house to hang out. You end up having sex with him in his friend's bathroom. It was good sex. You leave a few hours later. When you tell your sister what happened, she says he will never call you again because you had sex with him. But she is wrong. He calls you on New Year's Day. He says he enjoyed his time with you and wants to know if you want to go over to his house that night so he could cook for you. You usually don't do that but since you already had sex, you figure it would be fine to hang out at his apartment instead of going out. You feel special because he is going to cook for you. You go to his little basement apartment. You think, "At least he has an apartment." But he doesn't have a couch. He only has a mattress on the floor. He asks you to sit down on his mattress. Although you don't want to, you also don't want to seem rude, so you sit on his mattress and eat the food he cooked.

As you are sitting down listening to music he made, he warns you that you are going to smell something bad in a few seconds. He adds, "Just know it isn't me. It is the people upstairs flushing their toilet." Yes, he is right. You do smell something. It is something nasty. As the smell begins to settle down, a song he made comes on. The beat sounds really good so you start bopping your head to it. Little do you know, it is about him and his boys waiting for a hooker to come by. Just goes to show you that something that sounds good at first isn't always good. The words of the song are horrible and degrading. Not exactly your idea of a nice dinner. The combination of the smell and the lyrics of the song make your stomach hurt. You feel sick. You don't want to leave right away because you don't want him to think you are leaving because of the smell. You don't want to make him feel bad.

You end up falling asleep while waiting for him to fall asleep so you could leave, as he begs you to stay until he falls asleep. You wake up to a screeching noise near the pillow behind you. You open your eyes wide and are terrified to turn around and see what it is. You turn around expecting to see some kind of animal. It is him! He is grinding his teeth. There is an empty liquor bottle next to him and he is sleeping. You get up and leave. What a nightmare.

He used to work for off-track betting. This is ironic because your dad is a gambler, and he would tell you about all the degenerate gamblers he would see. You tell him about your dad and how he is probably one of them. When he ends up being laid off, you suggest he maybe work with gamblers who are in recovery. He thinks that is a great idea, as he tells you he always wanted to help people. Not too soon after you try to help him do you realize you should've been creating a plan to help yourself with your choice of men instead of trying to help him. He is just like the rest of the men you chose to be with.

One day, after you leave him, he calls you and says, "Why did you decide to have sex with me now and you wouldn't give me the time of day when we first met a few years ago?" You don't have an answer to his question. But you are glad he asked it because it made you realize that you should've gone with your first instinct and decided not to get with him.

Scenario Number Seven: You are out clubbing again one night during the summer with a friend from work. You are wearing a sexy gold dress that your friend calls the "Golden Globe dress." You stop at a diner and there is a sexy waiter there. You can't stop looking at him. When you leave the diner, your friend goes back in and gives him your number after you tell her you thought he was cute.

He calls you the next day and you start talking. You never hung out after that, but you always seemed to keep in touch through texts or calls. You had broken up with your boyfriend for three months and were single. Felix, the waiter, tells you he wants to come over and hang out when he finds out you moved closer to him. You contemplate it. You don't really want to hang out in your apartment because you don't want him to get the wrong idea. You would've much rather he took you out on a date. You tell him you will get back to him on whether you are going to chill with him.

In the meantime, your phone rings and it is your ex. He tells you he misses you and you hang up on him. You know he is no good for you. Deep down inside, you hope he will call back. When he doesn't call back, you call back and say, "If you missed me so much, why wouldn't you chase me or at least call me back, apologize, and offer to make it up to me?" His answer was in the form of a question: "Can I borrow your car? I don't really miss you. I just need your car to get my son to practice." When you say no in disgust, he hangs up on you again. Is he serious? How could he say that? You are devastated.

You cry your eyes out and decide you will hang out with Felix. It is something to do to get over things and try to feel better. When you tell him you will hang out, he asks you what you like to drink. You saw on his Facebook page that he loves to drink E&J so you tell him you like that, even though you had never tried it. He comes over and brings the biggest bottle of E&J you have ever seen. You drink it, not knowing how strong it is. He says he could not believe you like E&J and that he thinks you were made for each other because that was his favorite liquor. Little did he know you only picked E&J because it was on his Facebook page.

You get drunk and don't realize how fast it hits you. Felix starts trying to take your clothes off. After a while, he is successful in getting your pants off. You tell him to stop numerous times and try to pull away. He kisses you. He manages to stick his dick inside of you and you quickly push him off you. He finally stops trying. As you are lying there, the two of you start talking. You tell him you never have sex without a condom. Suddenly, you feel something wet. You get up and it feels like you peed yourself. You look over at Felix and he has a stupid look on his face. You ask, "Did you cum in me?" He said, "Yes, I did. By mistake. It must have been you pushing me away. When I finally got it, I couldn't handle it." You are so upset. You get up and take a shower.

He insists he doesn't have a disease and that he could not get anyone pregnant but that was not enough for you. Then, to make matters worse, he pulls out about twenty condoms and says, "Keep these. They are for next time. For every one condom there is, I am going to cum inside of you without a condom two times." You feel so disrespected.

When you talk to your friends the next day, they tell you that it sounds like you had been raped. You don't want to take it that far. You aren't sure if he liked you or if he had raped you. You don't know what to think. So, you leave it alone. You go to the doctor to get tested and take the morning-after pill. It was then that you decided that you would never hang out with a guy only because you are hurt over someone else or to get over someone else. You aren't only mad at Felix. You are mad at your ex for upsetting you and helping you decide to hang out with Felix due to his actions toward you. Most of all, you are upset with yourself for allowing that to happen.

As time goes by, Felix calls you and sends you messages telling you how he wants to see you. Just as you are thinking of responding one day after ignoring him for so long, you see a girl on his Facebook page. It says they are in a relationship. You ask him who she is, and he says he doesn't know what you are talking about. You wonder if their relationship started the same way yours did.

The only good thing that came out of the situation was that you now have a new drink of choice: E&J. You begin drinking it socially and your friends would make fun of you, saying they didn't know how you liked the taste and adding that it was a "man's drink." You want to be able to handle it so that no one will ever be able to get you drunk again.

A few months later when your ex-boyfriend contacts you again, you tell him about what had happened with Felix. Instead of him caring, he says, "Oh, man. What an asshole." You think, "That's it?" He has no sympathy toward the situation. It was then you realize you can't rely on him to help you through or understand. Even though your ex didn't ever do anything for you, you thought the one thing you liked about him was that he cared about you. You were wrong...About a lot of things.

You used to look at Felix's Facebook page from time to time and see pictures and comments of him and his girlfriend. The same girlfriend he had when he got with you. You used to ask yourself why he liked her so much and why he did that to you. Then, you decided it was time to stop. You not only delete him from Facebook but also from your life completely. The only thing you don't delete in your mind is the lesson you learned from the situation.

Scenario Number Eight: You go out with a guy you met in school. He has goals and is a hard worker, which are two qualities you also possess. You are out to dinner and having fun. Throughout the night, he compliments you on how pretty you are. After about the third compliment, he looks at you and says "I have been telling you how beautiful you are. Why haven't you told me I look handsome?" What is your answer? The answer to him is simple: "Why would I when we are talking about me?"

Scenario Number Nine: You meet a guy at an auto body shop. He takes you out on a first date and you have some drinks. After drinking three drinks of his own, he drives you home. The next time you go out, it is to the movies. You are early for the movie, so he asks you if you want to get a drink, and you do. As you are walking to the restaurant near the theater, he stops and says, "Will you be my Valentine?" You are a little (or a lot) taken aback, as it is only August. He then says, "I wanted to ask you before anyone else does." You tell him you must think about it, as you have only been on two dates. Then, he says, "I don't think we should get a drink because I don't want to drink and drive. You wouldn't do that, and I am sure you don't want me to either." The next words out of his mouth are, "So, since there isn't anything else to do, would you like to go..." As he said, "back to my car," you help him finish his sentence. He looks at you and says, "How did you know I was going to say that?" You think, "It comes along with years of practice and dating the same type of losers." You just smile and say, "I am just nice like that" as you walk into the doors of the movie theater to sit there and watch the previews with a big tub of popcorn. It beats making out with this loser in his car.

Scenario Number Ten: You are out with your friend when a guy comes up behind you and takes your drink, gulps it down, and hands you the cup back. You can't help but laugh. How bad could times be that a guy would do that? He asks you and your friend if you want to go out to eat after the club and you end up taking him up on the invite. After all, he does owe you a drink. When you get to the diner, he doesn't order anything, even though he said he was starving. You realize it is probably because he is broke (stealing your drink was a good indicator). When the bill arrives, it is $18.00. He takes out a ten-dollar bill and says he is going to the ATM for the rest. You are surprised he was going to pay. After about twenty minutes, you and your friend wonder what is taking him so long at the ATM and why he keeps printing so many receipts there. He comes back to the table and says, "The ATM is broke." You think to yourself, "No, you are broke." When he leaves to walk home, you try the ATM, and it works. You suddenly realize he needed a ride home so he offered to take you out to eat at a diner, a block away from his house, so he could get a ride home.

Scenario Number Eleven: You meet a handsome man through an online dating app. You go to breakfast at a diner close to your home for your first date. He lives in the next town over from your house. You hit it off immediately, there is chemistry, and you like how you feel while you are around him. You start dating. He doesn't always answer his phone. You suspect he may have a girlfriend, but you don't want to jump to conclusions without any evidence. So, you keep going on dates with him. One day, he comes to pick you up at your house. He comes in and puts his left hand on the wall and leans over to pet your cat. You notice a wedding ring. A million things are going through your mind, but you play it cool and don't say anything. He asks you if you have ChapStick and you tell him you only have lipstick. He goes to his car and gets ChapStick. While he is in his car, you start pacing back and forth in your house, feeling unsettled, deciding how to react next. When he comes back in, he is not wearing the ring. He then puts his ChapStick on your coffee table and says, "Please don't let me forget this here." You respond, "Forget what? Your wedding ring?" He says, "No, my Chapstick. I don't have a wedding ring." You let him know that you aren't feeling up to going out and he leaves.

Now, you have a reason to do some research. You google his name and voila, a picture of him and his wife with their baby registry appears! Not only is he married on a dating website, but they are expecting twins!

A few days go by, and he texts you, "Do you want to hang out?" You text him back, "Do you want to hang out?" He responds, "What time?"

You respond, "What time?" He says, "Why do you keep repeating what I'm saying?" You text back, "We must be twins." He responds, "I want to lick on your twins." Your final response is, "I want to babysit yours."

Some women reading these stories cannot relate. Either they are healed or have enough self-esteem to never give one of these idiots the time of day. I admire you if this is you and you never allowed abuse to enter your life. I also admire those who have allowed toxicity into their lives and have fought through it and survived, unscathed, like I did. Each of these scenarios happened to me in the past. As I look back, I am thankful for every one of these dumbass dudes, as they each were stepping-stones to help me heal and get to be the beautiful, confident, secure woman I have grown to become. Like many of you reading this, I also would never give any of these losers the time of day now. But my past, unhealed self unfortunately did. These are embarrassing and shameful stories to tell, but if one of them helps even one person, the shame and embarrassment of sharing the stories is well worth it.

Although many of us reading these stories would never accept this type of treatment, there may be some who have not quite reached their healing journey and who just may still be meeting these types of losers (I would refer to them as men, but these are not men-and there are unfortunately a lot of them out here). If you find yourself meeting these kinds of losers and enduring abuse, don't be too hard on yourself. Please know that it's not your fault. Be kind to yourself and know that you too can heal. To those women, I was once there too. I know what is toxic may also feel comfortable, but it is not healthy. It is imperative that you get comfortable being uncomfortable. The stories in this chapter and throughout the book reflect unhealthy relationships with unhealed individuals. My hope for you is that you dig deep down inside and find the strength to heal and no longer tolerate abuse or toxicity. It was so lonely when I was experiencing this pain and abuse. I felt unloved, unseen, unheard, and hopeless. No one seemed to understand why I stayed or why I continued to get into these abusive situations. I couldn't even understand. There was no one to tell me they loved me, no one who cared. I am here today to tell you that I love you, and I care. I want you to heal and to realize your worth. I want you to escape the torture and know that you deserve so much more. I pray that all the goodness that the world has to offer comes to you and that karma takes care of the rest.

CHAPTER TWELVE

Karma

I wish there was a fairytale ending for Ember with her prince charming where she gets married, has a family, and lives happily ever after. But there just isn't. She isn't married yet and is at an age where she is not sure if she will be able to have children of her own.

Although there was no fairytale ending in terms of a relationship with a man, Ember did heal and find self-love. She inspires others with her story, helps people through the work she does, and continues to heal herself in the process. She dates with intention, has learned from her past, and makes millions of dollars every year while living in her passion. Lastly, and most importantly, she is a dog mom to two Frenchie sons and is a soon-to-be dog mom to a newborn Frenchie daughter.

As for each of the men that she dated in the past, karma caught up with them, just as Ember's mother predicted it would, in ways that Ember could have never imagined.

Joseph: Married someone else and had three children with his wife, got the heart-shaped pool, just not with Ember

Nate: Died of a drug overdose on his 30th birthday

Rose: Got arrested with her husband for prostitution after luring a man over to their house to have sex and then beating the man up and robbing him. The craziest part of the story was her mugshot- she looks like a big, balding man, it's pretty disturbing.

Hector: Moved to Puerto Rico, became homeless, and then found another woman to support him and start a business for him. His daughter from his relationship with a woman before Ember ended up passing away suddenly

Oscar: He found Ember on a dating site fifteen years after they dated and asked her out again. She went out with him on one date and decided quickly that the date was a terrible idea. He was bragging about how he spent $900 on micro shading for his eyebrows, and he had to fluff up his pillow that he was using in his car several times during the drive to the restaurant (probably to ease the comfort of his hemorrhoids from all the butt sex he was having). When Ember ghosted him after the date, he reached out and asked why. When she told him that nothing changed and she wasn't interested in him, he said, "I know it isn't me, it must be something else." After thinking about it, Ember realized he was partly right. He was the same person all along, it was Ember who had changed and healed, and would no longer even think about entertaining that type of person.

Tyler: Ember stumbled across a picture of her and Tyler years later that she found in her garage. She couldn't help but wonder what she saw in him in the past, as she was way too pretty and good for him, and he wasn't as cute as she thought he was back then.

Anyway, his friend reached out to Ember twenty years later through a dating app and said, "Tyler said what's up?" Ember answered, "No thanks, not interested," to which his friend replied, "dammn." Some people never change. Fifty-something-year-old men still saying, "what's up? and having their friends ask, "wanna hang out?" All Ember can do is smile, knowing that she is currently living her best life, free of fuck boys like Tyler.

Keith: Went through desperate measures to reach out to Ember years later through several social media platforms to profess his love to her, just before Ember learned that he ended up marrying the mother of his ten children, finally! Ember prays they live happily ever after and that she never hears from him again!

Todd: Ended up going to prison for carjacking and is dating a man that he met in prison who he refers to as "Buffy." We would be remiss to not include how he impressed the world, or at least the town of Stupid Ville, by managing to get three DUI's in one night just days after being released from prison on the carjacking charges

Vincent: no updates, Ember hasn't heard from him (thankfully) and is too busy to care what he is doing

CHAPTER THIRTEEN

A Chapter for the Men of the World

Listen up, Gentlemen: You Have the Power to Make a Positive Difference. I know this book concentrates mainly on men who are not men but are instead cowards. But I do know and have met many genuinely kind, handsome men. Yes, I know they do exist.

For the men who behave like the men in this book, you should be ashamed of yourselves. Work to break the cycle. Do better. Get to the root of your problems so that the abuse doesn't continue. You have the power to change and to heal also. Choose to do better; gather the strength to get help.

I once saw a young boy in the store with his mother and he was crying. His mother turned around, got in his face, and yelled, "Stop it right now! Stop crying! Boys don't cry!" I couldn't help but think about the damage and impact that those words could have on that young boy later in his life. How he may become one of the men in this book who take their anger out on others and who don't know how to express their emotions. To the men of the world whose mothers or caregivers told them it's not okay to cry, I'm here to tell you that, not only is it ok to cry, but most women are also turned on by men who know how to express their emotions.

I do not know how men think or what makes them do the things they do. But I do know how I and many other women want to and deserve to be treated. I know that I appreciate a true gentleman who will talk things out. Maybe he must walk away temporarily to work through his emotions. But he comes back when he is ready and talks about it. He listens and isn't afraid to share how he feels. He doesn't walk ahead of his woman, he walks alongside her, holding her hand, and helping her to feel safe. I promise you that if you show your lady that you can not only take care of her needs but also have the strength to become emotionally intelligent, you will be irresistible. Men, my hope for you is that you heal from any childhood traumas and that you choose to do better than the stories in this book, way better.

Gentlemen, I wrote this book based on my experiences as a woman. But I do know that men can and have also been in abusive relationships. Women can be (and some are) abusive and toxic as well. I want all the men of the world to know that it is healing to rid yourself of toxic women and to find a woman who can appreciate all you have to offer.

My hope for the world of dating is that people are honest with themselves about what they want in a relationship and that they turn down anything that is not in alignment with their desires. To me, there is nothing worse than a man asking me to come over on the first date or talking about sex in the first conversation. I am aware that some women appreciate that, but that is such a turn-off for me. We must each work to be in tune with what we want and not accept anything less.

One day, after arguing with my boyfriend at the time, I stopped to get gas on my way home. Out of nowhere, the gas station attendant said, "Oh, sister- You are beautiful. Just remember you are expensive. Don't ever let anyone tell you different." He told me he had six sisters and could tell that I was "expensive." It was his way of saying I deserve the world and telling me not to settle for less than what I am worth.

The sad part was I didn't realize my self-worth at the time and that I really was "expensive." Instead, I would get used by others and give my hard-earned money and precious time to others who didn't appreciate me. I had to learn the hard way after years of suffering that I really am "expensive." I really am worth it.

The universe has ways of sending us messages and this was one I was grateful to hear. We are all "expensive" in our own way, and we should strive to see our worth daily. Let's uplift each other and build healthy, loving, lasting relationships. I challenge each of us to live life to its fullest and to treat ourselves and those around us with love and compassion.

Thank you and I hope you enjoyed reading my book

The End

Follow me on Instagram: gardenofe143

For videos and more stories,
subscribe to my Youtube: youtube.com/@opaswrld

www.ingramcontent.com/pod-product-compliance
Lightning Source LLC
Chambersburg PA
CBHW071117160426
43196CB00013B/2605